BOOK REPAIR

A How-To-Do-It Manual
for Librarians

KENNETH LAVENDER
SCOTT STOCKTON

HOW-TO-DO-IT MANUALS
FOR SCHOOL AND PUBLIC LIBRARIANS
Number 4

Series Editor: Barbara L. Stein

NEAL-SCHUMAN PUBLISHERS, INC.
New York, London

Published by Neal-Schuman Publishers, Inc.
100 Varick Street
New York, NY 10013

Printed and bound in the United States of America

Library of Congress Cataloging-in-Publication Data

Lavender, Kenneth.
    Book repair : a how-to-do-it manual for librarians / Kenneth
Lavender, Scott Stockton.
       p.   cm. — (How-to-do-it manuals for school and public
librarians ; no. 4)
    Includes bibliographical references.
    ISBN 1-55570-103-5
    1. Books—Conservation and restoration—Handbooks, manuals, etc.
2. Library materials—Conservation and restoration—Handbooks,
manuals, etc. 3. Bookbinding—Repairing—Handbooks, manuals, etc.
I. Stockton, Scott. II. Title. III. Series: How-to-do-it manuals
for school and public librarians ; no. 4.
Z701.L32 1992
025.7—dc20
                                          92-8109
                                             CIP

CONTENTS

SERIES EDITOR'S PREFACE

Book Repair: A How-To-Do-It Manual for School and Public Librarians is designed specifically for librarians working in small libraries or libraries with limited resources. *Book Repair* differs from other repair manuals available in its discussion of a wide spectrum of repair options, from basic techniques to alternative conservation treatments. At its core is the presentation of a series of decisions that you must make before beginning any treatment. Your answers to a series of questions will determine which treatment you choose for each book. Your choice will depend upon how important the book is to your collection, what kinds of resources you have available, and what expertise you have for a given type of treatment. *Book Repair* will help you choose the best possible treatment by balancing the needs of your library and the physical needs of the book.

Kenneth Lavender and Scott Stockton are both practitioners in the area of book repair and hand binding. Kenneth Lavender is Curator of the Rare Book and Texana Collections at the University of North Texas and adjunct professor of Library and Information Sciences, where he teaches courses in rare books, preservation, and binding.

Scott Stockton is Coordinator of User Services, Department of Academic Computing, Texas Woman's University. He is experienced in museum conservation practices and is a student of fine binding.

Barbara L. Stein
Series Editor

PREFACE

Book Repair: A How-To-Do-It Manual for Librarians explains basic book repair techniques useful to libraries with limited budgets, as well as alternative, and more ambitious, conservation treatments that might be considered by those with appropriate support. Repair techniques are shown for most of the common problems encountered in libraries: paper cleaning, paper mending, hinge and spine repair, and enclosures. Step-by-step instructions and clear illustrations are given for each treatment.

Book Repair is not intended to be a comprehensive manual of conservation techniques. It presents basic repair techniques within the context of decisions about your collections, staffing, expertise, support, and the needs of the repair object. This context of decisions is the underlying principle of *Book Repair*. Because of this focus, some techniques presented are more "expedient" than "conservationally sound." Where there is a question concerning the harmfulness of a suggested treatment, there will be a discussion of its possible consequences. If applied conscientiously and appropriately, the repair techniques described should achieve satisfactory results, but any technique, misapplied or poorly executed, may result in permanent damage to your book. Rare or valuable items should be evaluated by an expert before any action is taken. For further reference and discussion of repair and conservation treatments, a bibliography of recommended sources is included. In addition, sources for specific treatments will be suggested at the end of each chapter.

Your choice of the most appropriate treatment for a given book *must* be based on the decisions you have made concerning your collections, staffing, expertise, support, and the needs of the repair object. You must take into account the needs of the library, including circulation, retention, funds, time, and available expertise. In addition, you must consider the needs of the object, including intrinsic value, intellectual importance, physical condition, and use. These decisions lie along a spectrum of treatment options between basic repair measures and full conservation treatment. At one end you may have a current best seller that will be discarded after it has fallen apart or its popularity has waned; repairs for this type of material might be expedient and done with book tape and book glue. At the other end of the spectrum you may have a book of high monetary value, great importance to your collections, or unique content; you might consider full conservation treatment or at least evaluation by an expert.

For many school and public libraries, however, a large part of the collection lies somewhere in between; that is, a book is to be retained as long as possible but is not worth the expense that most conservation work entails. This problem has increased in recent years because publishers no longer keep a large inventory of titles in print, with the result that several types of publications, such as children's books, are no longer automatically replaceable. This situation brings many more common books into the realm of preservation with books that need to be treated for use far into the future.

The reader also needs to be aware that the field of preservation is a dynamic one, and its accepted knowledge is constantly changing. What was considered a safe technique only five years ago may now be questioned because of advanced scientific methods. In addition, there is often disagreement among experts about specific techniques. Sometimes this disagreement is based primarily on tradition, that is, where the person was trained and in what specialty. Sometimes, however, it is based on a new insight that has been gained from experimentation.

There are two types of book repair manuals currently available to librarians. First, major dealers in library equipment and supplies produce manuals that present easy-and-quick repairs using their materials. Many of the techniques are practical and the supplies are inexpensive, but the effects are irreversible and harmful. Second, several good conservation manuals have been published in the past decade, presenting sound techniques for book and paper conservation. Both types of manuals are useful for their specific circumstances, but these circumstances lie at opposite ends of the treatment spectrum. *Book Repair* will help you make decisions that balance the needs of your library with the physical needs of the object itself.

INTRODUCTION

Book Repair is designed as a manual rather than as a textbook so that each treatment chapter can stand alone. That is, Chapter 5, Protective Enclosures, is not dependent upon Chapter 2, Paper Cleaning. Before you attempt any of the treatment suggestions you should read thoroughly the Introduction and Chapter 1, The Basics: Tools and Techniques, for discussions on decision-making, principles of conservation, setting up a work space, and choosing the right tools, supplies, and equipment. This basic information is necessary for each of the subsequent chapters.

Tools, supplies, and equipment are also listed in Appendix A with their suppliers; the suppliers, their addresses, and telephone numbers are listed in Appendix B. Many supplies and tools, such as brushes, cloth, bone folders, rulers, and the like, may also be purchased at local art supply and school supply stores.

ORGANIZATION OF THE CHAPTERS

The introductory paragraphs of each chapter present the broad context of the treatment, the most common causes of the problem, and general instructions. The next section analyzes steps for making a repair decision and is divided into two parts: broad factors and specific factors. The former pertains to the larger context of any treatment, while the latter pertains to the specific one under discussion. The following broad factors are those that you must consider before beginning any repair work. All else depends upon them. These factors apply equally to all library materials.

DECISIONS

Importance of the item to the collections: How essential is this book to my library's collections? Has it been superseded? What is its usage pattern? Is another copy easily available? Do I have other titles to take its place?

Physical needs of the item: What condition is the item in? What is the strength of the paper? What can best be done for it?

Desired outcome of this repair: How long do I intend to keep this book? Is this repair only temporary until I can do something better? What are the consequences of the treatment I have chosen?

Time available for this repair: How long do I have to spend on this repair? Should I put it aside until I have others like it? Can I work it into my normal routine?

Personnel available for this repair: Who makes the decision about this repair? Am I the only person who can do this repair? Is there someone who can help me? Are there some steps I can leave to others?

Funds available for this repair: How much money is this repair going to cost? Is the repair affordable? How can I minimize the expenditures? Are there alternatives? What are the consequences if I have to postpone this repair until funds become available? Are there funds to photocopy the item?

Expertise available for this repair: What techniques do I know that might help me? Should I ask for outside help? Is this technique beyond my abilities?

Your answers to these questions will determine the type of treatment you decide on. You should think of these decisions as balancing one factor against another: What can I afford? What is best for the book? Very few repair decisions are completely straightforward. Usually a compromise between the desire to do right and the reality of the situation is necessary. Your choice of repair material, for example, depends upon how long you want the book to last. Page mends from plastic tape are strong but destructive; archival tape mends are strong but less destructive; heat-set tissue and Japanese paper mends are strong but not as destructive. The first are cheap and easy to apply; the second are expensive and easy to apply; the last are less expensive and substantially more difficult to apply. If you are going to discard the book after a short while, then plastic tape mends are obviously the most appropriate. If you are planning to retain the book in your collections, then you need to consider the latter alternatives. The same type of logic must support your decisions concerning all repair treatments.

The specific factors depend upon the nature of the material being repaired and must be considered in order to perform successful treatment. They might include fragility of paper, composition and coating of paper, type of tear to be repaired, size of object to be repaired. Equally important, however, are the consequences of the specific treatment under consideration for the condition of the object you are repairing. You need to define these factors before beginning the repair procedures.

SUPPLIES

Necessary supplies and tools are listed at the beginning of each repair procedure. Where appropriate, alternative choices will also be listed. Further discussion of tools and supplies is given at the beginning of each chapter and in Appendixes A and B.

PROCEDURE

Each repair procedure is presented in specific easy-to-follow steps. These steps take you from the beginning of the repair to the end, detailing each technique required and the materials needed. Please follow the steps exactly in the order they are presented. After you become proficient in these techniques, you will find that many of the steps come naturally and that many of the techniques are used again and again in different procedures.

ALTERNATIVE CONSERVATION SUGGESTIONS

This section introduces possible conservation alternatives for objects that are of exceptional value and importance. These alternatives are discussed only as options for the professional conservator. You need to become familiar with the limitations of book and paper repair treatments and alert to factors requiring the help of a professional conservator.

There are, however, three principles that are basic to all conservation treatments and should be kept in mind even in basic repair decisions. Your decisions must balance these principles with the needs of your collections and the book itself. Again, this may be a trade-off between expedient and conservationally sound techniques.

Harmlessness: The repair should never harm the object itself. Many basic book repair materials are eventually harmful, especially those with adhesives. These include hinge and spine tape, paper mending tape (except for archival tape), book glue, labels, and covers.

Durability: The strength of the mend should never be greater than the strength of the material mended. An obvious disregard of this principle is seen in many hinge repairs where heavy stiff tape or cloth has caused the pages to break against it. Having said this, your mend should be durable enough to provide protection throughout the desired life of the object.

Reversibility: The basic principle of conservation is: Do not do anything you cannot undo. An acknowledgment of the importance of this concept is the marketing of *reversible* glue and mending tape from the large library suppliers. Some adhesives are reversible with water; others with organic solvents. You should be aware, however, that many conservators doubt whether these adhesives are completely reversible.

These three principles should become factors in your treatment decisions. Book tape is harmful, strong, and irreversible. It is also inexpensive and easy to use. How do these qualities apply to the specific book I have to make a decision about? Do I have any alternatives? Often one or more of these principles must be set aside even by conservators. The most professional restoration treatment is not completely reversible without harm to the original book, nor is it meant to be. The materials and techniques used are selected because of their durability and harmlessness and are expected to last the life of the book. Here, also, it is a question of balancing factors to fit the specific situation.

FURTHER READINGS
The final section of each chapter directs you to specific sources listed in the Bibliography that offer further information on similar or alternative repair techniques, supplies and materials, and conservation issues.

1 THE BASICS: TOOLS AND TECHNIQUES

What You Need and
What You Need To Know

Before beginning work on any book repairs, you should set up a suitable work space. Whether it is small or large, simple or elaborate, the work space is made up of three basic components: bench area; lighting; tools, supplies, and equipment. (See Figure 1.)

BENCH AREA

Most professional book repairers prefer to work standing up for better leverage and control. A surface of approximately 6 feet by 2½ feet is adequate; the height should be comfortable for working. Many laboratories use steel-legged tables placed in adjustable wooden blocks. Wooden bar stools or adjustable secretary chairs should be available as seating. The surface should be resistant to scratches and easy to clean such as a laminate or formica. If only wood is available, suitable coverings can be purchased or made from materials at your local building supplies dealer.

In addition, adequate storage for supplies is essential. Many book repair stations have a large pegboard at the back to hold tools, as well as built-in shelves for different sizes of paper, bookcloth, and the like. However, large and heavy items, such as stacks of binders' board or barrier board, should be stored horizontally to help prevent warpage.

For many school and public libraries, such a professional work station is not feasible. Fortunately, any large, flat surface can be adapted for a book repair station. In fact, the work surface need not be dedicated solely to book repair, although this would be preferable since you would not have to move your materials at inconvenient times. A 6- by- 2½-foot folding table or a cafeteria table would be suitable. Again, the surface should be resistant to scratches and easy to clean.

There are also inexpensive ways to accommodate the storage of tools and supplies. A tiered carrousel sold for kitchen

FIGURE 1   Bench Area and Tools Needed for Repairs

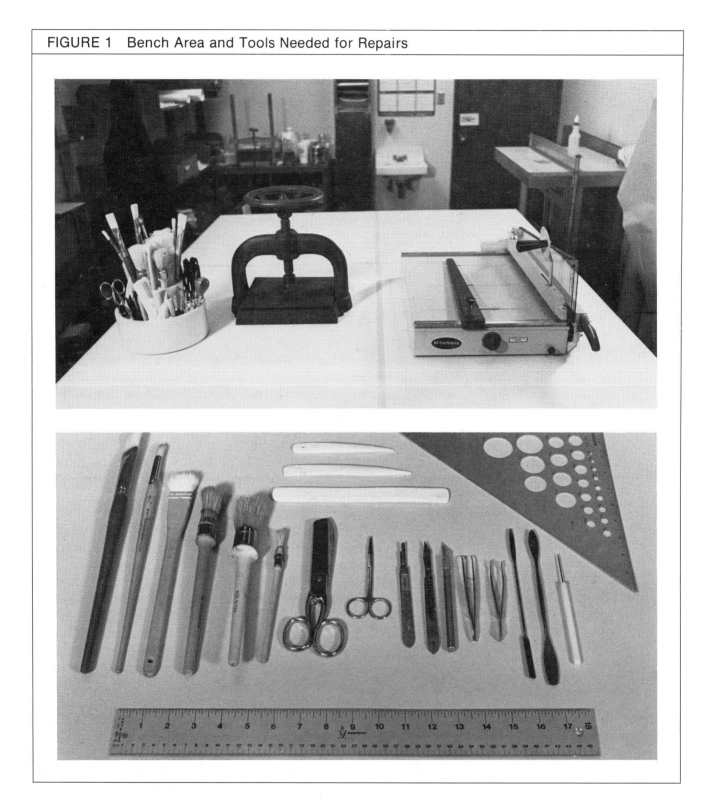

gadgets is handy for holding tools. It is high enough for long-handled brushes, and the individual compartments allow quick access to the different tools. A plastic desk or kitchen drawer separator makes a suitable storage container for scalpels, blades, knives, and other sharp objects. Margarine tubs (with lids) are good for holding glue and paste (both raw and made); an empty liquid detergent bottle makes a handy glue container; mayonnaise jars are good for mixing paste; an empty one-pound coffee can makes an adequate brush holder. Paper and bookcloth may be stored in drawers or on shelves in a closet.

You will also need to provide storage for any large equipment you are using. Most commonly this would include a paper cutter, book press, and a dry-mount or laminating machine. As you become more advanced in book repair, you may consider purchasing a board chopper (board shear), mat cutter, and a phase box maker.

Access to a sink is a necessity for any book repair station. You will need it for cleaning brushes and containers, and for providing water for making paste and for clean-up. Access to a stove or microwave is also needed. (A hot plate may be used if it is the only available appliance.) These do not need to be located within your work space, but they should be nearby.

LIGHTING
Natural light is best for any book repair work space. Besides giving the least distortion, it provides a good work atmosphere. In many libraries, however, windows are reserved for public areas, while the work areas are entirely windowless and artificially lighted. Flourescent tubes, which are inconsistent and distorting, are the most common source of light. Your work station should thus also be provided with an incandescent *task lamp*, which gives off a concentrated light and can be easily moved to best advantage.

TOOLS, SUPPLIES, AND EQUIPMENT

Your choices for tools, supplies, and equipment are dependent upon your treatment decisions. For most basic book repair, for example, your decisions may dictate the most easily obtainable items at the least expense. For the best conservation treatment, however, your decision must be judged against the three criteria of harmlessness, reversibility, and durability. Fortunately, as library supply dealers become more aware of and concerned with preservation needs, an increasing number of tools, supplies, and equipment are satisfying these two extremes. That is, many *conservation alternative* items are now easily obtainable and within the budget constraints of most school and public libraries. Consequently, acid-free products are now more commonly available, as are buffered papers and reversible adhesives and tapes. When at all possible, prefer these *conservation alternative* products to those that will eventually cause harm to your books.

Tools, supplies, and equipment that are needed for a broad range of book repair treatments are listed below. Many are used for more than one treatment, and several are basic items used for any repair work. A brief statement is included where we feel that you may need direction in selecting the proper type. Suppliers for most items are listed in Appendix B.

TOOLS

Bone Folders: Use genuine bone. Both an 8-inch rounded and a 5-inch to 6-inch pointed one are needed.

Brushes: It is best to have an assortment of brushes. The four most useful are the oil painting brush (with a small flat tip), a Japanese watercolor brush (with a pointed tip), a glue brush (with a round tip), and a hake brush (a broad flat tip). All come in various sizes and are readily available from art supply stores. In addition, a long-handled dusting brush is useful for clearing your work space of eraser particles and dirt.

Dissecting Needle: A stiff needle in a wooden or plastic shank. Used in making small holes or in scoring Japanese paper. Available where laboratory supplies are sold. A good ice pick may also be used.

Glass or Plexiglass: Small pieces (approximately 3 inches by 3 inches) are used as or with weights. In addition, a large piece of glass (8 inches by 14 inches) may be used for pasting-out and other repair activities.

Knitting Needles: Metal, #1 and #6. Used in hinge repair.

Knives and Blades: A scalpel or X-Acto® knife is essential for many repairs. A heavier utility knife is needed for cutting boards. A kitchen paring knife is also useful. Scalpel blades #22, #23, and #25 are the most used for book repair work. A handle #4 will be needed for these blades.

Micro-spatula: A thin double-bladed spatula, useful for applications of small amounts of glue and for other repair procedures. Available where laboratory supplies are sold.

Rulers: It is good to have an assortment of rulers, from 12 inches to 36 inches, with at least one that is cork-backed. A heavy metal ruler may also be used as a straightedge.

Scissors: Two sizes are needed—a standard pair and a small pair, such as embroidery scissors.

Sewing Needles: Chenille needles are good for sewing with linen book thread.

Tacking Iron: A small heating iron used with heat-set tissue and labels. It must have a heat regulator, built-in or attached.

T-square or Triangle: You need some method of making square corners and perpendicular cuts. T-squares are useful for squaring large pieces of paper and board, while triangles are better for smaller applications.

Tweezers: An assortment is best, including one blunt-nosed pair, one straight sharp-nosed pair, and one curved sharp-nosed pair.

Weights: Both small and large weights are necessary. They may be bean bags, cloth filled with shot, paper weights, or bricks covered with felt.

SUPPLIES
Bookcloth: Many types of bookcloth are available, including library buckram, cotlin, and linen. Virtually all are acceptable and should be chosen according to your structural, aesthetic, and financial needs.

Board: The most common are barrier (phase box), binders',

COMMON SUPPLIES TO HAVE ON HAND

- Cleaning Cloth (e.g., One-Wipe®)
- Cotton Swabs
- Double Boiler
- Glass Dishes (various sizes)
- Kleenex
- Masking tape
- Paper Towels (undyed)
- Pencils (#2 or harder)
- Rags (soft cotton)
- Sandpaper (fine grade)
- Waste Paper (e.g., old phone books)
- Wax Paper

bristol, and mat board. Boards come in varying thicknesses and weights.

Cleaning Pad: There are several brands available from conservation and art supply stores (Charvoz, Lineco, Opaline).

Cloth: Closely woven unbleached muslin, linen, cambric, or jaconet are used in hinge and spine repair.

Erasers: You will need at least four types for your repair work: kneadable rubber, art gum, plastic or white vinyl, and compound.

Glue: Many suppliers are now offering acid-free book glue along with their regular products. Although it is somewhat more expensive, it is preferred for books that you intend to keep. The most widely available type of book glue is PVA (polyvinyl acetate). Under certain applications and with difficulty, it may be reversible with water or acetone. Avoid using other types of glue, such as rubber cement, since they are harmful to books and irreversible.

Heat-set Tissue: A finely woven tissue with a heat-activated adhesive. Used with a tacking iron, it is reversible and virtually invisible. Because of economy and ease of use, it should be considered for paper mends on general collections. In addition, it is needed for mending coated papers where water cannot be used.

Nonwoven (spun) Polyester: Also known generically as release cloth and spunbonded polyester, it is used where you need a non-stick surface. The most widely available are Reemay® and Hollitex®.

Papers: Several kinds of paper are necessary for book repair. Your assortment should include blotting paper, endsheets, silicon release paper, and several weights and shades (off-white to beige) of Japanese paper.

Paste: For archival mending use either rice or wheat starch. Mix one part starch to four parts water in top of double boiler. Let stand for five minutes. Cook over simmering water until paste becomes thick and transluscent. Remove to glass or plastic container and let cool. You may vary the proportions for a thinner or thicker paste. Also, the longer you cook the paste the thicker it will become.

Polyester Film: This film is commonly known as mylar, even though Mylar® is actually a registered product name from duPont. It is not a plastic but an inert polyester that is used for bookwraps and jackets and for encapsulation. It comes in various thicknesses, but the 3 mil (.003 inch) is the most versatile. It is important to buy Mylar®D because it is the most stable form available. Another acceptable polyester film is Melinex®516 from the ICI Corporation.

Book Tape: Book tape comes in a wide variety of styles, colors, and strengths. It is also cut into specific shapes, such as wings. For basic spine repair and strengthening of paperbacks, you will need several of the types commonly available from library suppliers. They are, however, irreversible and may eventually cause deterioration of your book.

Tape For Paper: There are also several types of tape available for mending paper, the most common of which is Magic® Transparent Tape. They are the most economical mending products and are for use on books that you do not intend to keep. They are, however, irreversible and will eventually cause deterioration of the paper.

Tape For Archives: Document repair tapes that are archivally safe yet easy to use have recently become widely available. They include Document Repair Tape by Ademco and Filmoplast®P. They are preferable to regular paper mending tapes, but they are considerably more expensive.

Double-sided Tape: For encapsulation and other procedures you will need to have 3M Scotch Brand®415 double-sided tape. This is the only type of double-sided tape that is acceptable for these procedures. The ¼-inch-width tape is recommended.

Thread: Irish linen binders' thread of medium weight (18/3) is needed for sewing signatures and pamphlets.

EQUIPMENT

Board Shear: A heavy-duty precision cutter for binders' board, barrier board, and heavy paper. This is an expensive piece of equipment, but it is essential if you are going to create your own hardback books, case bindings, or boxes.

Book Press: There are several kinds available, but they are generally suitable only for smaller books. Large books can be pressed through the use of weights and wooden boards.

Corner Rounder: An expensive item but very helpful if you make a lot of phase boxes.

Laminating Machine: Most school libraries have one. They are excellent for protecting flat materials that get a lot of use but are expendable. It is important to remember, however, that the heat from the laminating process actually initiates the destruction of the paper the process is meant to protect. When in doubt, prefer encapsulation.

Paper Cutter: Most school and public libraries have a good paper cutter. It is essential for cutting all types of paper but may also be used for polyester film and thin barrier board.

Phase Box Maker: Also called a *crimper,* its sole purpose is to make the creases for phase boxes. These creases may also be made with a bone folder and straightedge, but if phase boxes are a major part of your storage procedures, this expensive machine can save a lot of time.

BASIC STRUCTURE OF COMMON BOOKS

It is important to have a basic knowledge of a book's fundamental structure in order to understand how your repairs fit in with and affect the item you are working on. Figures 2a and 2b will help you visualize the structure as we describe it. You may also, of course, study a book that has come apart, noting its similarities and differences. Binding terms that are used in this manual (and in many other repair books) are printed in italics.

The form of our common book is called a *codex* and is essentially a group of leaves hinged at the back and put between two covers. Researchers believe it originated with the hinged waxed tablets used by secretaries in Rome, was picked up by the early Christians for use in group readings, and was refined by monks for copying and preserving texts. The codex form was prevalent by the fifth century and has remained virtually the same since that time. Only the materials have changed, not the form.

Books are printed on large *sheets* of paper, which are then folded into *gatherings* or *sections* (often incorrectly called *signatures* or *quires*). From this process comes the *format* of the book (e.g., folio, quarto, octavo), which also indicates the number of *leaves* in each gathering. Thus, a quarto has four leaves. In a regularly sewn book, each gathering is sewn through its middle onto *tapes* or *cords*, or simply loop-stitched to the next

---

FIGURES 2a–2b   Inner and Outer Book Structure

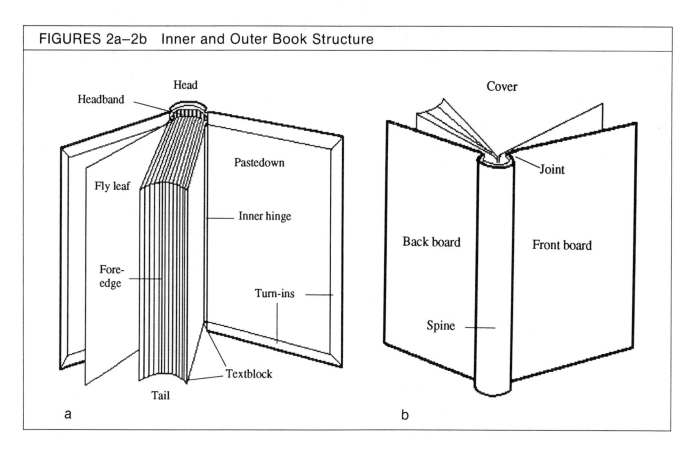

a

b

section; the *thread* appears between the two middle leaves. Once all the gatherings have been sewn in order, the *end-sheets* are attached. This forms the *textblock*. The *spine* is then glued and a piece of cloth called the *super* is attached to it to provide strength. Sometimes *headbands* are pasted onto the spine. Spines may be flat or rounded; if they are rounded they are said to have *shoulders*. The *joints* of the *cover* fit into the shoulders of the textblock. Also attached across the spine onto the *boards* is some type of *hinging cloth*; in some instances the super may serve as the hinging cloth. In either case, the cloth is what affixes the textblock to the cover. The most common type of cover is called a *case* and is made up of two boards and a single piece of *bookcloth*. The hinging cloth is pasted onto the boards, and the outer leaf of the endsheet (called the *pastedown*) is pasted onto each board. The inner *hinges* of a book are between the pastedowns and the *fly leaves*.

In a *perfect* binding the folds of the gatherings have been sheared off and the individual leaves glued to the spine (as in most paperbacks) or to a piece of super (as in some children's and art books). This is why the leaves drop out when the spine is cracked. This type of binding is very difficult to repair, because there are no tapes or sewing to attach anything to. If the binding margins are wide enough, the textblock may be *oversewn*, which causes problems in opening the book. Otherwise, it can only be reglued. A better type of perfect binding is the *double-fan adhesive* binding, in which the glue is actually spread on both sides of the leaves, allowing the book to lie open more easily.

Many of the repair techniques in this manual have been developed for the codex form of book. If you take a while to familiarize yourself with the basic elements of this structure, much time and effort will be saved later on.

GRAIN

Another aspect of binding and repair materials that you will need to become familiar with is *grain*. Grain refers to the direction of the fibers in paper, board, and cloth. Sometimes paper and, particularly, cloth have a grain pattern woven into or embossed on the material. This pattern may or may not be the same as the direction of the actual grain of the material, so you must examine the physical makeup of the piece you are working with.

Paper, board, and cloth are much more flexible *along* the grain; therefore, it is important that the direction of the grain be *parallel* to the spine of a book. This will allow the book to open and close easily and will reduce stress at the hinges. In addition, these materials swell and stretch as atmospheric conditions change. If the grain is running *across* the book, that is, parallel to the head and tail, the hinges of the book will eventually crack. Once you have determined the direction of the grain, mark an arrow lightly in pencil to remind yourself.

PAPER

There are four ways to determine grain in paper. All the methods will cause some damage, and are therefore listed here from least to most abusive. Thick paper is easier to examine than thin; large sheets are easier than small pieces.

1. Lay a sheet of paper on a flat surface. Bend it over one way and measure the height of the curl. Bend it over the other way and measure again. Because paper is much more flexible along the grain, the shorter curl will indicate the direction of the grain. This method works particularly well with large sheets of paper (see Figure 3).
2. Wet one corner of the sheet of paper. Since paper shrinks and stretches along the grain, the direction of the *inside* of the curl will indicate the direction of the grain.
3. Make a small crease on one side of the paper near a corner. Make another crease on the other (perpendicular) side. The crease will be easier to make and much sharper along the grain.
4. Make a small tear on one side of the paper near a corner. Make another tear on the other (perpendicular) side. The tear will be easier to make as well as straighter and cleaner along the grain (see Figure 4).

BOARDS

Although most boards used in repair work (e.g., barrier, binder's, mat) do not show a grain pattern, they all have a grain direction as part of their structure. The differences show up

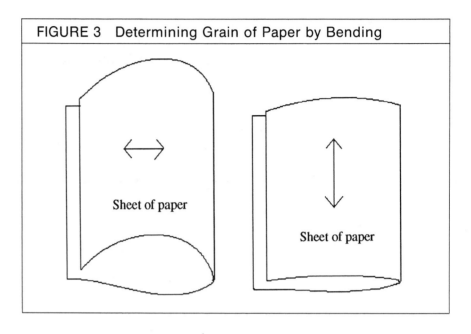

FIGURE 3   Determining Grain of Paper by Bending

Sheet of paper

Sheet of paper

not only in the composition of the boards, but also in their weights and thicknesses. Thick boards are harder to bend, but thin boards are more difficult to examine because they bend so easily. The different types of board, however, may all be examined with the following method.

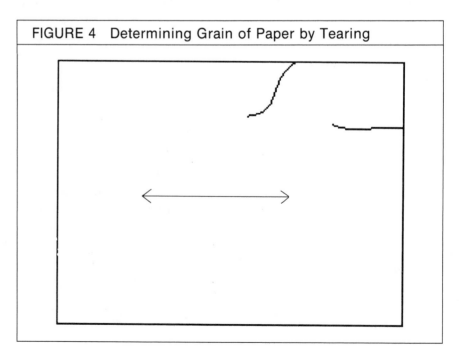

FIGURE 4   Determining Grain of Paper by Tearing

FIGURE 5a Bending Board Against the Grain

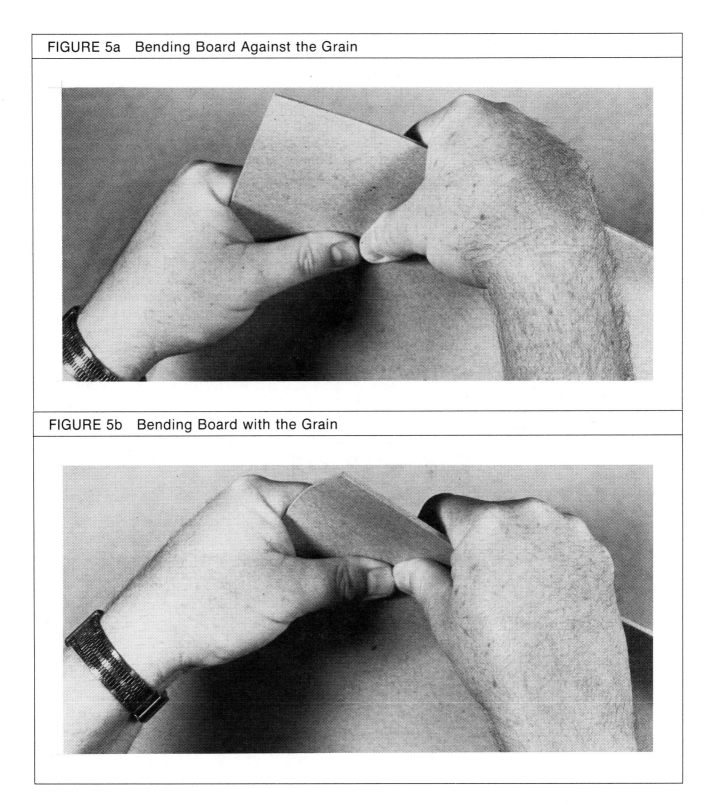

FIGURE 5b Bending Board with the Grain

1. Place your hands on opposing sides of a board equidistant from the corners; your thumbs should be touching.
2. Gently pull the board forward with your fingers, first one side, then the other. The board will bend more easily and further along the direction of the grain (see Figures 5a and b).
3. Very thin boards may also be bent over and measured, or creased, as with paper.

CLOTH

Cloth can be deceptive because of its pattern. Many book cloths have a pattern that shows a definite *grain*, but its direction is not necessarily the same as that of the actual grain (or warp). By far the best way to determine the grain (or warp) of cloth is to find the selvage (the smooth strip running down opposite sides). For most machine-made cloth the grain (or warp) is *parallel* to the selvage. Unfortunately, many times the selvage no longer exists because the cloth has been cut into pieces. In this case, you may try the methods recommended above for determining the grain of sheets of paper or very thin boards.

FURTHER READINGS

Bench Area, Tools, Supplies, and Equipment:

Greenfield, pp. 34–59, *et passim.*

Kyle, pp. 23–29.

Morrow, Appendix 3.

Adhesives and Paste:

Kyle, pp. 44–49.

Ritzenthaler, pp. 100–102.

Basic Structure of the Common Book:

Greenfield, pp. 1–19.

Horton, frontispiece and pp. 9–20.

Grain:

Greenfield, pp. 22–26.

2 PAPER CLEANING

Paper in books may become soiled from a number of causes: dirty fingers, markings, accidents, and normal air pollution. Each type of soil has its peculiar properties and may require different methods of cleaning. Most common in library books is soil caused by markings and dirt. Unfortunately, certain types of markings are virtually impossible to remove. For example, with ball-point pen and crayon marks you may be able to remove the surface components, but the stain will remain. For marks that contain grease, such as fingerprints, you may be able to remove the dirt, but the grease will remain. In fact, there is no known cleaning agent, wet or dry, that will completely remove grease or oil from paper.

There are *wet* and *dry* methods of cleaning paper, but for the person engaged in normal book repair only the *dry* methods should be attempted. Even in using these dry cleaning agents it is important to keep in mind that paper is fragile and that its surface is easily scratched or torn. This is particularly true with coated papers, such as those used in art books and encyclopedias. It is thus imperative that you begin with a cleaning powder, which is the least abrasive cleaning agent. If the dirt or mark still remains, you may progress through the various kinds of erasers discussed later in this chapter. And, as with all things done to paper, test a small unobtrusive spot first. Cleaning agents should be used only on the white areas of the page, not on the print or other images.

As with all repair techniques, you can facilitate the cleaning process and make the best use of your time by separating books according to the type of cleaning method needed.

DECISIONS

The following factors will influence your decision regarding the most appropriate repair treatment. These factors address first the broader context of the item, then the specific problem(s) to be treated.

BROAD FACTORS

Importance of item to the collections

Physical needs of the item

Desired outcome of this repair

Time available for this repair

Personnel available for this repair

Funds available for this repair

Expertise available for this repair

SPECIFIC FACTORS

Type of mark or stain

Composition and coating of paper

Fragility of paper

CLEANING POWDERS

Cleaning powders are the least abrasive form of cleaning agent and are very good for such problems as dingy appearance, smudges, and general dirt marks.

SUPPLIES
Document cleaning pad (Charvoz, Lineco, Opaline)

PROCEDURE
1. Sprinkle a small amount of cleaning powder (about three twists of the bag or a good pinch of loose powder) over the dirty area. If using a document cleaning pad, twist the pad until the proper amount of powder drops out. Do *not* rub the pad itself on the paper. Clean only a small area at one time.

2. Using the flat part of your fingertips, rub gently with a circular motion. Do not apply force with the ends of your fin-

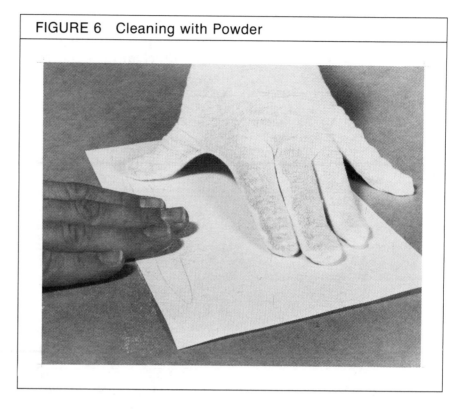

FIGURE 6   Cleaning with Powder

gers. If you are cleaning near the edge of the paper, be careful not to catch the edge and tear it. Rub gently until the powder looks grey or dirty (see Figure 6).

3. Using a soft brush, sweep the dirty powder off the edge of the paper. Make sure that there is no powder caught under the paper, as this would cause damage to the underside of your document.

4. Continue with clean powder. If the area does not become clean after a few applications, do not try to rub harder. This will only damage the paper. Progress to the next cleaning agent, the eraser.

ERASERS

Erasers come in a variety of types and are made from a variety of materials. They range from low abrasive (kneaded rubber and gum erasers) to high abrasive (White Pearl®). They are made of gum, rubber, plastic, or a compound. The appropriate kind depends on the type of dirt or mark you are trying to erase and the importance of the book you are trying to clean. As with all cleaning agents, use the least abrasive eraser first and clean only a small area at one time. Avoid using a high abrasive eraser on delicate or coated paper.

SUPPLIES

Following is a list of erasers from the least to the most abrasive.

Kneaded rubber erasers (Eberhard Faber®) are excellent for surface dirt. In place of this eraser, a commercial paper cleaning compound such as Absorene may be used.

Gum erasers (ArtGum®, Star): are used for pencil marks on delicate paper.

Plastic and vinyl erasers (Magic-Rub®, Staedtler) are used for pencil and graphite marks on paper and film.

Compound erasers: Pink Pearl® is used on pencil; White Pearl® is used on ball-point ink.

PROCEDURE

Follow these steps to clean paper with kneaded rubber erasers:

1. Remove wrap and knead eraser until it is pliable. Pull off a small piece and knead into a ball. The kneading will help the eraser to become tacky.
2. Dab the eraser ball onto the dirt or mark. Do not rub. It will pick up surface particles without leaving a visible residue. It is particularly useful in removing loose graphite, chalk, and charcoal.
3. Gently brush dirt particles off eraser, and replace it when it becomes dirty or rough.

The following procedures should be implemented when using all other erasers:

1. Rub gently in one direction with small, gentle strokes, being careful to hold the edge of the paper down with your fingers. Work towards the edge of

FIGURE 7   Cleaning with an Eraser

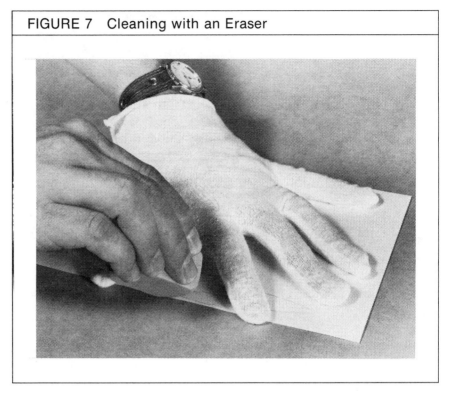

the paper (see Figure 7). Do not rub back and forth. This only damages the paper.

2.   After several strokes, brush residue off edge of paper, making certain that the particles do not remain on your work space.

3.   Feel the paper. If it has become rough, this means that you are removing the paper's surface along with the mark. Although it is often impossible to avoid this, the paper is being weakened and is in danger of tearing.

ALTERNATIVE CONSERVATION SUGGESTIONS

Paper objects whose value and condition merit extensive cleaning treatment may be candidates for *wet* cleaning techniques. These techniques must be attempted only by trained conservators, because of the extreme danger they present to paper of all kinds. In general, they may include the application of water and, sometimes, chemicals; dipping in a tray or placing on a suction table; the possible application of deacidification and buffering agents. The decision to consider such a treatment rests on the importance and value of the object, the condition of the paper, the possible harm to the paper or image, and the cost of conservation.

FURTHER READINGS

Greenfield, pp. 62–64

Horton, pp. 30–35.

Ritzenthaler, pp. 95–98.

3 PAPER MENDING

All paper objects are susceptible to wear along folds, tears along the edges, and losses, both intentional and accidental. While some tears seem minor, it is important to repair these in order to stop further damage when the item is used again. Losses, too, must be repaired in order to prevent further loss. Tears and losses in paper objects can be mended with a repair tape, with heat-set tissue, or with Japanese paper and a paste made from either rice starch or wheat starch. Variations of these methods provide solutions to a wide range of paper mending problems.

It is important to prepare the document to be mended before the repair is begun. If the repair is in a map or flat document, it is best to flatten the object before repairing it. In many cases, this can be done by placing the item between clean sheets of blotter or other paper, then pressing this package under boards and weights. If the repair is in a book, it is a good idea to place a clean piece of thin board or blotter paper under the leaf that is to be repaired. If there are small gaps in the tear, lay a piece of wax paper or release paper between the board and the leaf to be repaired. Large gaps may require a tape mend on both sides of the tear, or an insert mend, using the same techniques employed to repair losses.

DECISIONS

The following factors will influence your decision regarding the most appropriate repair treatment. These factors address first the broader context, then the specific problem(s) to be treated.

BROAD FACTORS

Importance of the item to the collection

Physical needs of the object

Desired outcome of this repair

Time available for this repair

Personnel available for this repair

Money available for this repair

Expertise available for this type of repair

SPECIFIC FACTORS

Type of tear to be repaired

Size of object to be repaired

Number of printed sides on the paper to be repaired

GLUE AND PASTE MENDS

The simplest way to repair a tear in a piece of paper is by gluing or pasting the torn edges back together. This can be done only when the torn edges of the paper are beveled to some extent. Torn edges are said to be beveled when one edge of the tear overlaps the other edge (see Figure 8). This overlap may be glued or pasted. Therefore, this type of mend is not possible if the paper has been cut rather than torn. It is not even possible on every tear, as some tears in papers simply do not have a bevel.

The polyvinyl acetate (PVA) or paste that you use for this type of repair should be rather thin. If you are using PVA, dilute it with approximately 3 parts PVA to 1 part water. PVA is difficult to reverse, however, and thus should not be used on archival or valuable objects. There is a great deal of variation in the thickness of paste, making formulas somewhat less accurate. However, if you used the paste formula in Chapter 1, dilute the resulting paste with 2 parts paste to 1 part water.

SUPPLIES

PVA or paste	Blotting paper
Small glue brush	Reemay®

FIGURE 8   Beveled Tear

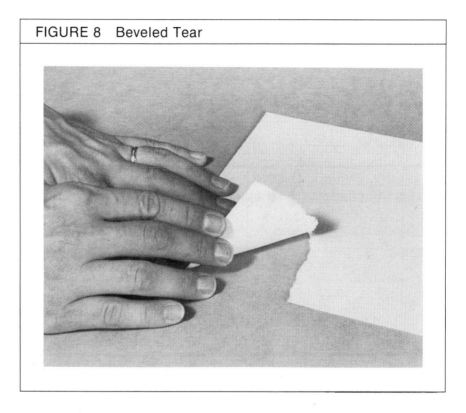

PROCEDURE

1. If you are using PVA, place a piece of wax paper under the torn page. If you are using paste, use a piece of Reemay® and a piece of blotting paper. Be sure to line up the bevels of the tear before you begin this procedure. The edges of some tears will fluctuate along the length of the tear, with first one edge on top, then the other (see Figure 9a).

2. Gently lift one torn edge and spread the thinned PVA or paste on the bevel of the other edge (see Figure 9b).

3. Lay the bevel of the raised edge down on the glued bevel and carefully tap the tear to tack the bevels together. Then place a piece of Reemay® on each side of the mended paper and blotting paper on the outside of the Reemay® (see Figures 9c and d). Gently smooth the repair with a bone folder.

FIGURES 9a–d   Mending Paper with Glue or Paste

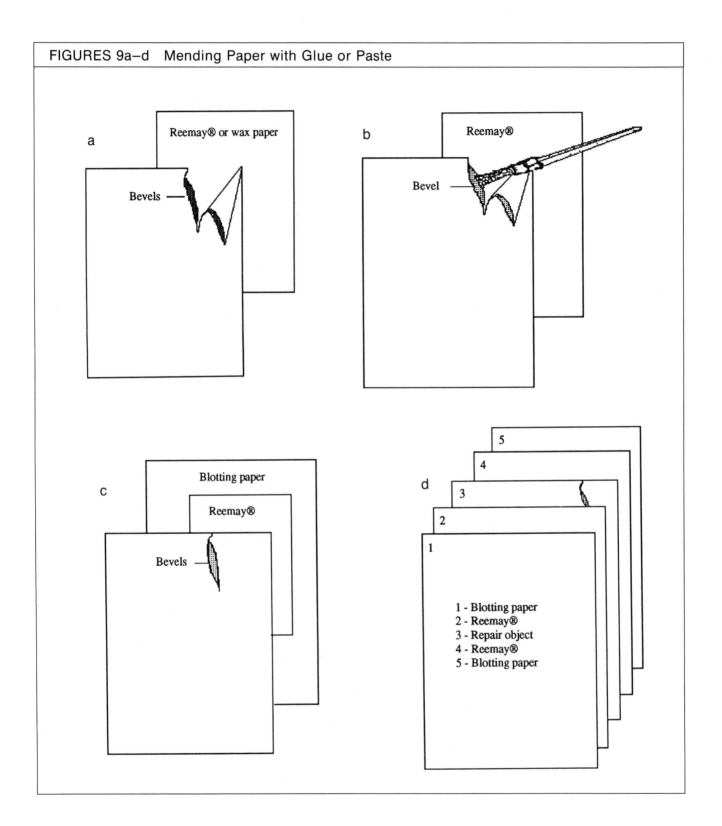

4. Place the repaired paper, with the blotting paper and Reemay® under weights and allow the PVA or paste to dry. If you are using PVA, most manufacturers suggest an hour drying time. Drying time for paste varies according to the exact mixture used and the length of cooking time, but most will dry overnight.

TAPES

Tape can be used on virtually any type of tear, although it is not recommended for items of artistic, archival, or historical value. Such items should be repaired with one of the more archival methods of paper mending. However, if you need to mend a tear in one of several paperback copies of a best seller that will be discarded in a few months, tape is both suitable and economical.

Tape is not only versatile, but it is also the simplest and most economical tool for repairing tears in paper. Of course, there are different types of tape from which to choose. Document repair tape is the most archival tape available, sold under the names Filmoplast® P and Document Repair Tape, and costs approximately 15 cents per foot. 3M Scotch® Magic Transparent Tape, on the other hand, costs approximately two cents per foot. 3M Scotch® now offers Magic Plus #811, a removable transparent tape that costs only three cents to four cents per foot, allowing a somewhat more archival repair without a great expense.

SUPPLIES

> Tape (preferably, though not necessarily, an acid-free repair tape such as Filmoplast® P)
>
> Bone folder
>
> Small piece of polyester film
>
> Metal ruler
>
> X-Acto® knife or scalpel

PROCEDURE

1. Line up the torn edges to be repaired. Be careful to follow the bevels of the tear.

FIGURES 10a–c

MENDING PAPER WITH TAPE

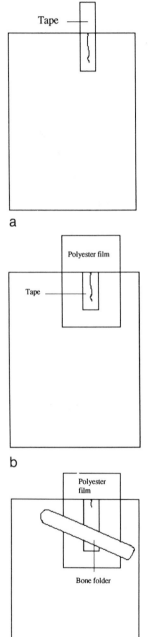

a

b

c

2. Tear off a piece of tape as long as the tear. If repairing an edge tear, you can use a piece twice as long as the tear, folding it around the edge of the paper to strengthen the mend on both sides. Make the fold in the tape slightly beyond the edge of the paper. This precaution will prevent possible damage to the edge of the paper.

3. Gently place the piece of tape on the tear. Carefully tack the tape in place, starting at one end of the repair and working to the other end. If you are repairing an edge tear, fold the tape just past the edge of the paper and continue putting the tape in place over the reverse side of the tear (see Figure 10a).

4. When the tape is in place, lay the polyester film on the repair and use the bone folder to gently rub the tape through the polyester film (see Figures 10b and c).

5. When the tape is firmly affixed to both sides of the paper, use the metal ruler and X-Acto® knife or scalpel to trim any tape that overhangs the edge of the paper. Not all repairs will require this step.

SIMPLE MENDS WITH HEAT-SET TISSUE

Items that require a more archival repair should be repaired with heat-set tissue. This is a simple and economical process, once you have made the initial purchase of tools and supplies. Variations of the repair can be applied to losses as well as tears and cuts. For example, large losses or corner losses can be repaired with heat-set tissue by cutting one piece of tissue or paper to fit inside the loss and another, slightly larger piece to be placed on one or both sides to hold it in place.

SUPPLIES

Heat-set tissue

Tacking iron

Silicon release paper or a non-woven polyester film such as Reemay®.

Embroidery scissors

Pencil

Gum or kneaded rubber eraser

Metal ruler

X-Acto® knife or scalpel

PROCEDURE
1. Preheat the tacking iron to medium.

2. Line up the torn edges to be repaired, being careful to follow the bevels of the edges of the tear.

3. Place a piece of heat-set tissue, shiny side down, over the tear.

4. Use the pencil to lightly mark the outline of a piece of heat-set tissue that is exactly the size and shape needed for the repair. This piece of tissue should extend $\frac{1}{8}$ inch to $\frac{1}{4}$ inch beyond the tear on all sides.

FIGURE 11   Tacking Heat-Set Tissue with Tacking Iron

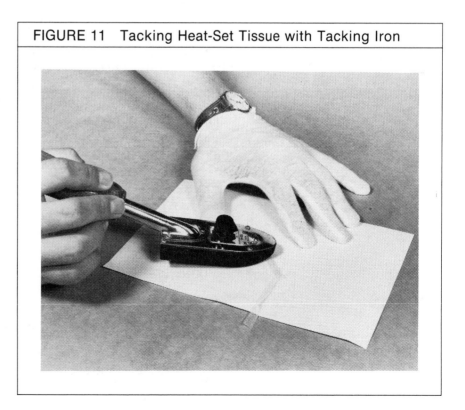

5. Lift the heat-set tissue from the object and use the scissors to cut out the piece needed for the repair. After this step, be sure to erase the pencil marks.

6. Place the heat-set tissue on the tear; again, the shiny side should be down. Cover the tissue with the Reemay® or silicon release paper.

7. Lightly rub the tissue with the heated tacking iron, gently moving the iron over the repair. When the heat-set tissue is almost invisible, it should be firmly adhered to the paper (see Figure 11).

8. Using the ruler and X-Acto® knife or scalpel, trim any tissue that extends beyond the edges of the paper.

REPAIRING LOSSES WITH HEAT-SET TISSUE

Losses in the pages of a book or other pieces of paper take three basic forms. Some losses occur along the edge of a piece of paper; others occur at the corner; still others occur in the center of the page, usually the result of vandalism. While each of these types of losses requires slightly different treatments, many of the same techniques can be applied to their repair; therefore, all of these treatments will be described as one. The basic procedure utilizes three layers of repair material. A filler piece is cut to fit in the loss, and a layer of heat-set tissue is applied to both sides of the page in order to hold the filler piece in place.

SUPPLIES

Heat-set tissue

Tacking iron

Silicon release paper or a non-woven polyester film such as Reemay®

Embroidery scissors

Pencil

Gum or kneaded rubber eraser

Metal ruler

X-Acto® knife or scalpel

PROCEDURE

1. Preheat the tacking iron to medium.

2. Place a piece of filler paper under the loss in the page or sheet of paper to be repaired. This filler paper should be approximately the same thickness as the torn page. If possible, it should be close to the same color as well.

3. Holding the torn page firmly down on the filler paper, lightly trace the outline of the loss on the filler paper. Remove the filler paper and cut out the insert piece with the small scissors. Cut along the outside edge of your line to get the best fit. Gently erase the pencil mark with the gum or kneadable eraser. If you are repairing an edge loss, allow the insert to extend beyond the edge of the paper. If you are repairing a corner loss, allow the insert to extend beyond both edges of the paper.

4. Place a piece of heat-set tissue with the shiny side down over the loss (see Figure 12a).

5. Use the pencil to lightly mark the outline of a piece of heat-set tissue that is exactly the size and shape needed for the repair. This piece of tissue should extend ⅛ inch to ¼ inch beyond the tear on all sides. Again, if you are repairing an edge or corner loss, allow the tissue to extend beyond the edges of the paper.

6. Lift the heat-set tissue from the object and use the scissors to cut out the piece needed for the repair. Use this piece as a pattern to cut another piece of heat-set tissue that is shiny on the opposite side, or repeat steps 5 and 6 for the opposite side of the torn page. After this step, be sure to erase the pencil marks (see Figure 12b).

7. Carefully aligning the edges, place the insert into the loss and place one piece of heat-set tissue with the shiny side down

FIGURES 12a–d   Mending a Corner Loss with Heat-Set Tissue

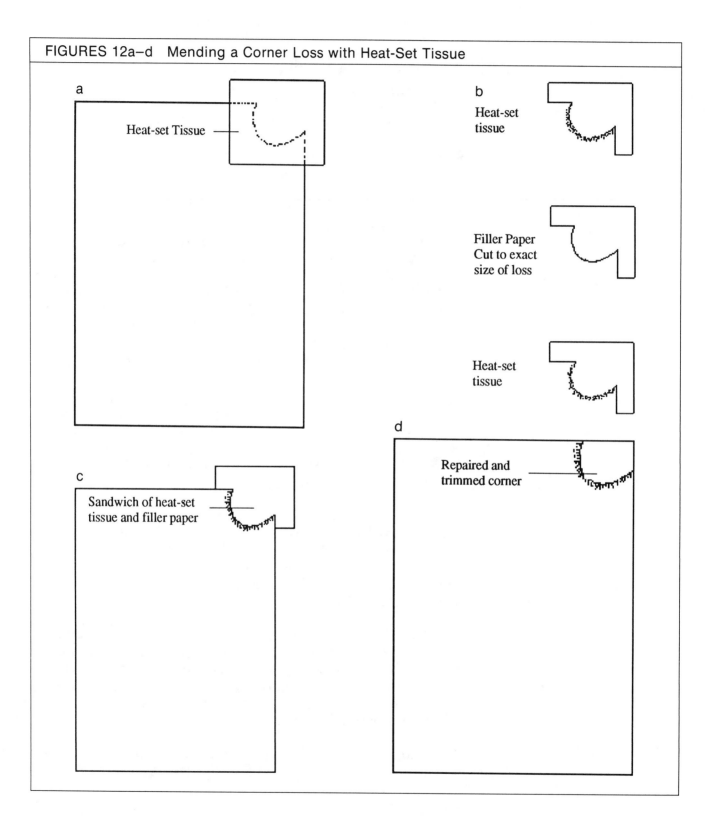

a

Heat-set Tissue

b

Heat-set
tissue

Filler Paper
Cut to exact
size of loss

Heat-set
tissue

c

Sandwich of heat-set
tissue and filler paper

d

Repaired and
trimmed corner

on the insert, allowing the edges to overlap the loss equally. Then cover the tissue with the Reemay® or silicon release paper (see Figure 12c).

8. Lightly rub the tissue with the heated tacking iron, gently moving the iron over the repair. When the heat-set tissue is almost invisible, it should be firmly adhered to the paper.

9. Turn the page over, place the other piece of heat-set tissue on the loss, and cover with Reemay® or silicon release paper.

10. Repeat step eight for this side of the page.

11. If you are repairing an edge or corner loss, you will need to trim the filler paper and tissue that extend beyond the edges of the paper with the metal ruler and X-Acto® knife or scalpel (see Figure 12d).

TIPPING-IN

One particularly useful type of paper mending is the tipping-in of leaves that have come loose or have been torn out. In a few instances, tape can be used for tipping-in. However, it is not recommended unless there is a stub left to which the leaf may be taped (see Figure 13). When a leaf is taped directly to the edge of another leaf, the second leaf will often tear out as well. Heat-set tissue is also a possibility when tipping-in, but it is not recommended either, simply because it is very difficult to get a tacking iron all the way into the gutter of a book. The best adhesives for tipping-in, therefore, are paste or PVA. Both can provide a strong, permanent repair that is also easy and economical. It is important to remember that the materials used in tipping-in, as with other repair treatments, depend upon the decisions you have made concerning the book's value and importance to your collection.

SUPPLIES

Adhesive (tape, paste or PVA)

Metal ruler

FIGURE 13   Torn Leaf and Stub

X-Acto® knife or scalpel

Reemay® or wax paper

Glue brush

PROCEDURE

1. A leaf can be torn out of a book in many different ways, each creating a different set of problems. If a narrow, easily accessible stub was left along the gutter of the book, merely line up the edges of the torn out page and the stub in the book, then repair with tape. If you do not wish to use tape, you can use the same techniques described earlier for mending an overlapping tear with PVA or paste.

2. If the leaf was torn down into the gutter at one or more points along the spine, you must prepare the book and the torn out page. Whatever scraps of a stub were left in the book should be trimmed to an even line if there is enough of the

FIGURE 14   Trimming the Stub

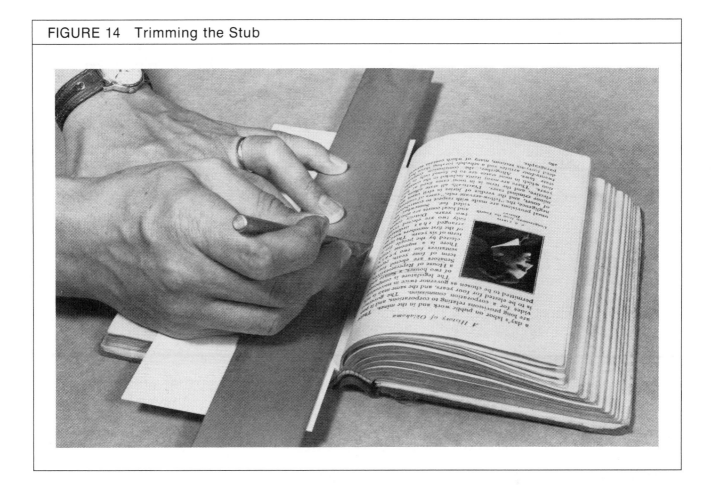

stub left to do this (see Figure 14). Also, the spine edge of the leaf should be trimmed to a straight line that is perpendicular to the top and bottom edges of the page (see Figure 15a). This can be difficult and sometimes impossible if, for instance, the tear curves into the print area of the page. In such a case, trim as far as possible without removing any print and repair the rest of the tear using one of the methods suggested in this chapter. (Note: If the leaf was torn down into the gutter all along the spine, it is best to find the other leaf in the section to which it was attached. Depending on the construction of the book, this second leaf may need to be tipped-in as well.)

3. If more than $\frac{1}{8}$ inch has been trimmed from the page, it is best to attach a hinge to the spine edge of the page. This hinge can be of paper taped to the page or of Japanese paper attached with starch paste (see Figure 15b).

FIGURES 15a–d   Tipping-In a New Page

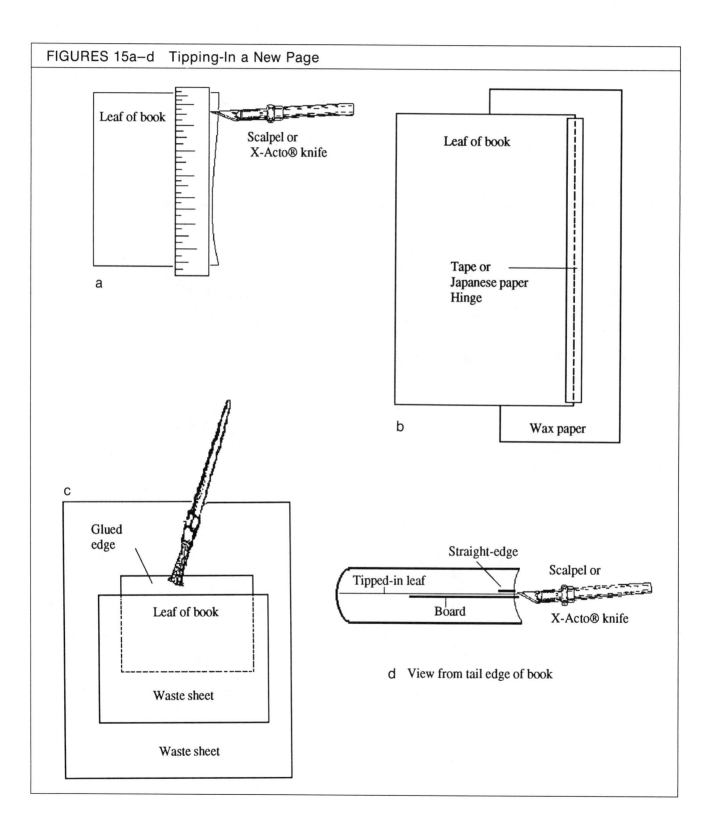

Leaf of book

Scalpel or
X-Acto® knife

a

Leaf of book

Tape or
Japanese paper
Hinge

b

Wax paper

c

Glued
edge

Leaf of book

Waste sheet

Waste sheet

Straight-edge

Tipped-in leaf

Scalpel or

Board

X-Acto® knife

d   View from tail edge of book

4. The leaf, with its hinge if necessary, should be placed face down on a piece of mylar or waste paper. Another piece of mylar or waste paper should be placed on top of the leaf, allowing $\frac{1}{16}$ to $\frac{1}{8}$ inch of the spine edge of the leaf to extend beyond the edge of this waste paper. If an entire leaf or pair of leaves has fallen out of the book, this and subsequent steps can be used with no previous preparation of the leaf or leaves.

5. While firmly holding the top piece of mylar or waste paper in place, spread paste or PVA along the protruding spine edge of the page (see Figure 15c). See Chapter 1 for more information regarding the properties of paste and PVA.

6. Carefully line up the edges of the leaf with the edges of the textblock, and press the hinge edge against the leaf behind it. If the tipped-in page extends beyond the fore edge of the textblock, trim off the excess paper. This can be done by placing a piece of waste board under the leaf and a metal ruler on top of the leaf. Line the ruler up with the fore edge of the textblock and trim along the ruler with the knife. Remove the board and ruler (see Figure 15d).

7. Insert a release layer such as Reemay® or wax paper on both sides of the tipped-in page. Close the book and weight it, allowing the paste or PVA to dry overnight.

JAPANESE PAPER AND STARCH-PASTE MENDS

The previously described methods of mending tears in paper objects are suitable for most of the paper mends needed in a library; however, Japanese paper and starch paste offer an alternative. This is an archivally sound process that can be done at a very reasonable cost. Also the techniques involved can be mastered without too much difficulty and are useful in spine repair as well as paper mending. Therefore, it will be discussed in full for the more advanced book mender, but it is still recommended that items that are particularly delicate or that are of greater artistic, bibliographic, or historic value be left to a professional conservator. It is also recom-

Figure 16

MENDING STRIP OF JAPANESE PAPER WITH EDGES FEATHERED

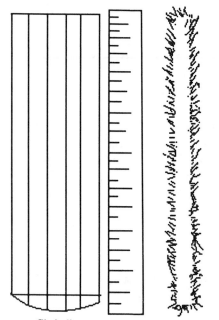

Chain lines

mended that you practice on unimportant papers before you attempt a repair with Japanese paper and starch paste.

For items that are not adversely affected by moisture, Japanese paper and starch paste provide the strongest, most archival repair. It can even be used to repair losses, using the same techniques described previously for repairing losses with heat-set tissue. Japanese paper comes in many weights and in many shades of beige or off-white. If you intend to do this type of repair often, it is best to keep an assortment of weights and shades of colors best suited to the types of items you repair. If you only intend to do this type of repair occasionally, it is more economical to purchase only the paper you need for each repair. If you intend to repair large losses or corner losses, Japanese paper is particularly useful. Because it comes in such a wide variety of weights, a paper that is as thick as the paper to be repaired can be used for the insert, and a thin paper can be used on the outside.

In order to mend tears with Japanese paper and starch paste, you will need to know how to tear Japanese paper and how to make starch paste. (A recipe for starch paste can be found in Chapter 1.) The Japanese paper should be torn instead of cut in order to allow some of the the long fibers of the paper to extend beyond the edge of the torn strip. This utilizes the long fibers of the paper to their best advantage and makes the edge of the repair less noticeable. It is important that you fan out the long fibers with a soft, dry brush after you tear the paper. If the Japanese paper has chain lines, it is important to tear the paper parallel to these lines (see Figure 16). If there are no chain lines, tear the paper along the grain.

There are three methods of tearing Japanese paper. The first of these methods, and the best for very thick papers, involves laying a metal ruler or straightedge parallel to the chain lines or grain direction at the point you want the tear. A small, pointed brush is then dipped in water and gently run along the straightedge, leaving a thin, moist line on the paper. The paper is then folded up around the straightedge. The straightedge is removed and the paper is gently torn along the wet fold (see Figures 17a-d). The second method of tearing Japanese paper is most useful with medium weight papers. In this method also, you lay a metal ruler or straightedge along the line you wish to tear. Holding the straightedge firmly, lift up on one end of the paper and slowly tear it along the straightedge. The third method of tearing Japanese paper also utilizes a straightedge placed along the line to be torn. Holding the straightedge firmly, gently drag an ice pick or dissecting needle along the straightedge, scoring the paper. Then remove the straightedge and gently pull the strip away from the paper along the scored line, being sure to draw out the long fibers (see Figures 16 and 17d).

SIMPLE MENDS WITH JAPANESE PAPER

SUPPLIES

Japanese paper

Rice or wheat starch paste

Metal ruler and X-Acto® knife or scalpel

Blotting paper

Nonwoven polyester such as Reemay®

Ice pick or dissecting needle

Paste brush

Micro-spatula

Small tweezers

Bone folder

Small weights

Pieces of glass or plexiglass

Waste paper or scraps of polyester film

Small pointed brush

PROCEDURE

1. Find a mending paper that is appropriate for the paper to be repaired. The two papers should be approximately the same color and weight. If possible, the mending paper should be just a bit lighter in weight than the paper to be repaired.

FIGURES 17a–b   Using the Water Method to Tear Japanese Paper

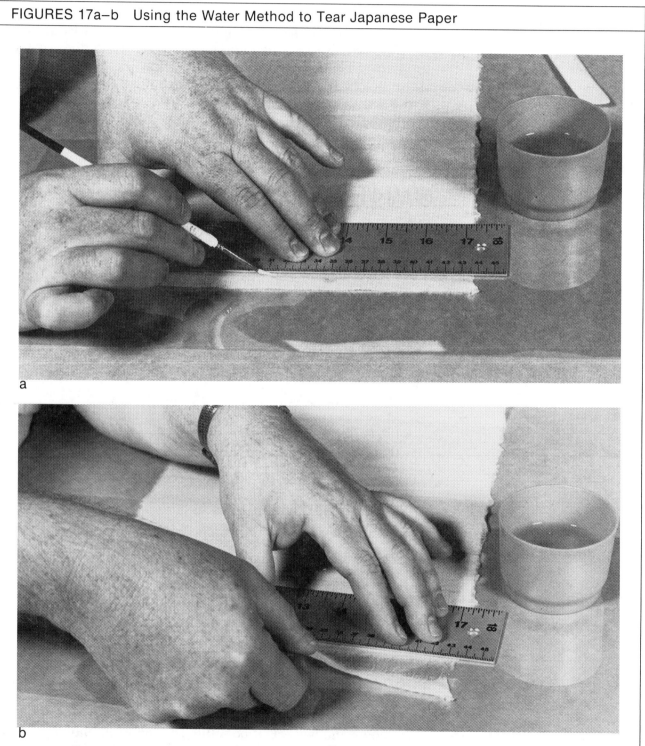

a

b

FIGURES 17c–d   Using the Water Method to Tear Japanese Paper, Cont.

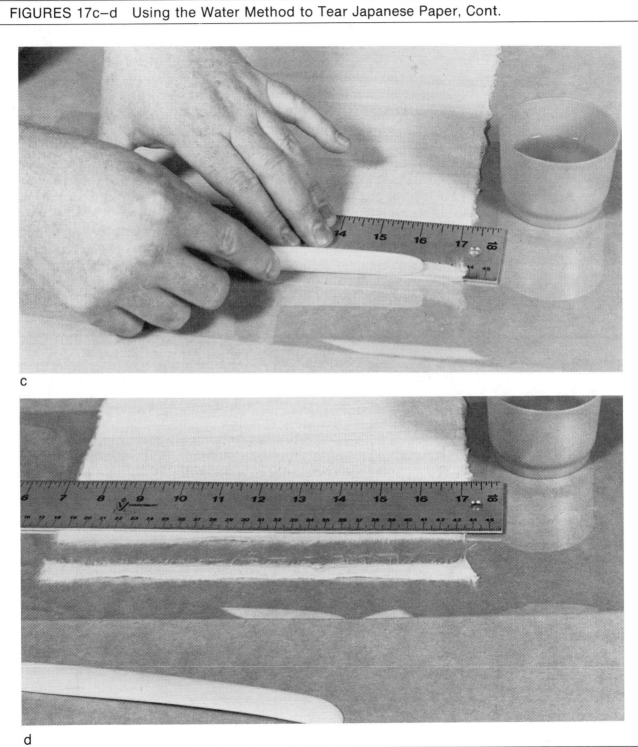

c

d

2. Using one of the methods described above, make a mending strip about ¼ inch longer than the tear and wide enough to extend approximately ⅛ inch on either side of the tear. The torn edges of this strip should be parallel to the chain lines in the Japanese paper.

3. Line up the torn edges to be repaired, being careful to follow the bevels of the edges of the tear.

4. Spread paste evenly over the piece of wax paper or polyester film. If less moisture is desired on the mending strip, you can paste out on a piece of blotting paper instead. Lay the mending strip in the paste on the waste paper. Place a piece of waste paper over the mending strip and gently rub the paper with a bone folder to coat the Japanese paper with paste.

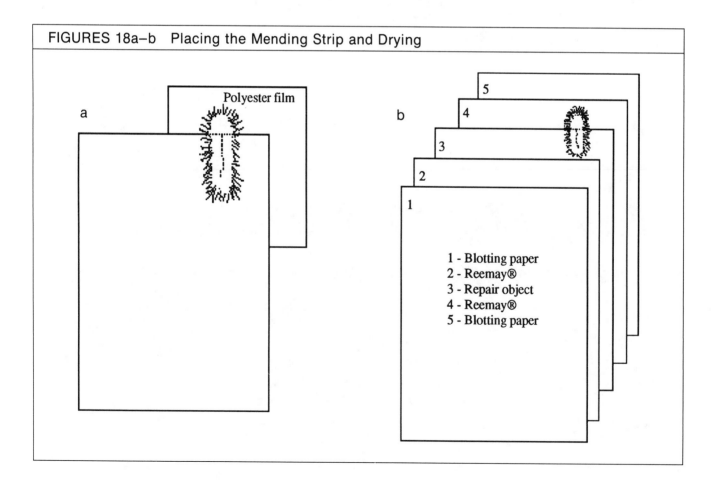

FIGURES 18a–b   Placing the Mending Strip and Drying

a

Polyester film

b

1
2
3
4
5

1 - Blotting paper
2 - Reemay®
3 - Repair object
4 - Reemay®
5 - Blotting paper

Remove waste paper and gently lift the mending strip out of the paste using the micro-spatula or tweezers. Do not lift too quickly or the strip will stretch, which will cause the mend to wrinkle as it dries.

5. Lightly place the mending strip over the tear and gently press it down onto the paper (see Figure 18a).

6. Carefully lift the mended paper and slide a piece of blotting paper under the mended area. Place a piece of nonwoven polyester on each side of the mend, and another piece of blotting paper on top of that (see Figure 18b). Put a piece of glass or plexiglass on top of the blotting paper, and, finally, place a light weight on the glass.

7. In 15 to 30 minutes, lift the weight and change the blotting paper on both the top and bottom of the repaired paper. Be sure to leave the Reemay® in place. Then allow the mend to dry overnight.

8. Remove the weight, the non-woven polyester, and the blotting papers and, using the metal ruler and knife, trim the mending strip to the edge of the mended paper if necessary.

ALTERNATIVE CONSERVATION SUGGESTIONS

Of course, further conservation alternatives are available to the professional conservator. Crumbling maps, for example, can be lined with Japanese paper and starch paste. Some adhesives, such as Lascaux, are heat activated like heat-set tissue, but can be used with any paper or cloth. A conservator should also be consulted if, for any reason, you need to reverse a paper mend. While some tapes, such as Filmoplast®P, can sometimes be peeled up from the paper if pulled very slowly, removal of tapes and heat-set tissue should be left to the conservator. Japanese paper and starch paste mends can usually be reversed with water or very thin paste, but this, too, should be left to a conservator.

FURTHER READINGS

Repairs with Paste or Tape:

Greenfield, pp. 74–77.

Kyle, pp. 54–56.

Repairs with Heat-Set Tissue:

Morrow, pp. 113–116.

Tipping-In:

Greenfield, pp. 91–103.

Kyle, pp. 59–65.

Repairs with Japanese Paper and Starch Paste:

Kyle, pp. 56–58.

Morrow, pp. 102–112.

Ritzenthaler, pp. 102–105.

4 HINGE AND SPINE REPAIR

The hinges and spines of books are particularly susceptible to damage from frequent use, careless handling, and even from book drops. Such treatment results in damage to both inner and outer hinges and to the spine itself. When this damage occurs in casebound books with cloth bindings, it can be repaired easily and inexpensively. While some of these procedures can also be performed on casebound books with paper bindings, this is not recommended. Paper is a more delicate material than bookcloth, and deteriorated paper is even more delicate.

Most library vendors offer a variety of materials for the repair of hinges and spines. These materials include items like rolls of buckram strips that are two inches to four inches wide. These can be very useful for replacing spines. These materials also include such items as hinging tape in both single- and double-stitched versions. Because these tapes are made of a heavy tape and adhesive that will be attached to the paper of the textblock, they will eventually cause the paper to tear along the edge of the tape. Therefore, they are not recommended for books you wish to keep in your collection.

This chapter is divided into two sections, the first discussing procedures for the repair of casebound books with cloth bindings, the second discussing the strengthening and repair of paperbound books.

DECISIONS

BROAD FACTORS

Importance of the item

Physical needs of the object

Desired outcome of this repair

Time available for this repair

Personnel available for this repair

Money available for this repair

Expertise available for this type of repair

SPECIFIC FACTORS

Extent of damage to hinge(s) and spine

Type of binding

Overall condition of binding

Importance of original cover

SECTION 1: CASEBOUND BOOKS

Most of the hardbound books in your library have a case binding. A case binding consists of two boards and a spine piece made as a single unit, which is attached to the textblock. Most of these bindings utilize bookcloth or paper for the covering material, though some use leather. Because paper and leather bindings are more difficult to repair, these bindings should be left to a bindery or conservator. Most cloth covered books, however, can usually be repaired in the library, unless they are of greater archival or monetary value. The textblock is usually sewn on tapes or recessed cords, but sometimes the sections of the textblock are merely stitched together. Sometimes the tapes are placed into grooves on the boards, but in other cases they are simply glued to the inner surface of the boards under the super. Occasionally, the tapes are cut off at the edge of the textblock, as is usual with recessed cords. While this practice results in a weaker binding, it is a binding that is more easily repaired.

TIGHTENING LOOSE HINGES

This procedure is useful when the textblock is sagging in the boards, but the hinges have not torn away.

SUPPLIES

PVA in a tall, thin bottle such as a liquid detergent bottle

Metal knitting needle (longer than the book)

Bone folder

Glue brush

Wax paper

Figures 19a–c

TIGHTENING A LOOSE HINGE

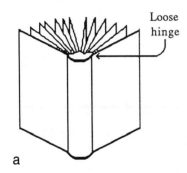

a

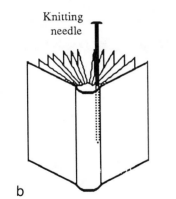

b

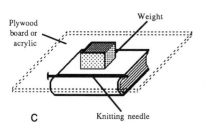

c

PROCEDURE

1. Stand the book on the table with the boards spread wide enough to hold the book up. Gently pull the textblock away from the spine, but do not tear the hinges (see Figure 19a).

2. Dip the knitting needle into the PVA bottle, being sure to coat the needle with glue.

3. Carefully avoiding the spine, insert the knitting needle into the gap between the loose endsheet and the board of the case (see Figure 19b). If both hinges are loose, repeat this process for the second hinge.

4. Close the book, lay it flat, and use the bone folder to push the outer hinges down in the joint. Turn the book over and repeat for the other hinge if necessary.

5. Place wax paper between the boards and the textblock and place the book under weights. A knitting needle can be placed in the outer groove of any hinges that were tightened to help keep them stable while the glue dries. Be sure, however, to use clean needles (see Figure 19c).

REPLACING ENDSHEETS

Often you will have books with tears in one or both endsheets along the inner hinge (see Figure 20). These books can be repaired by replacing the torn endsheet with new paper. Endsheets are available in pre-folded, pre-cut sizes. See Chapter 1 for more information regarding paper for endsheets.

FIGURE 20   Example of a Torn Endsheet

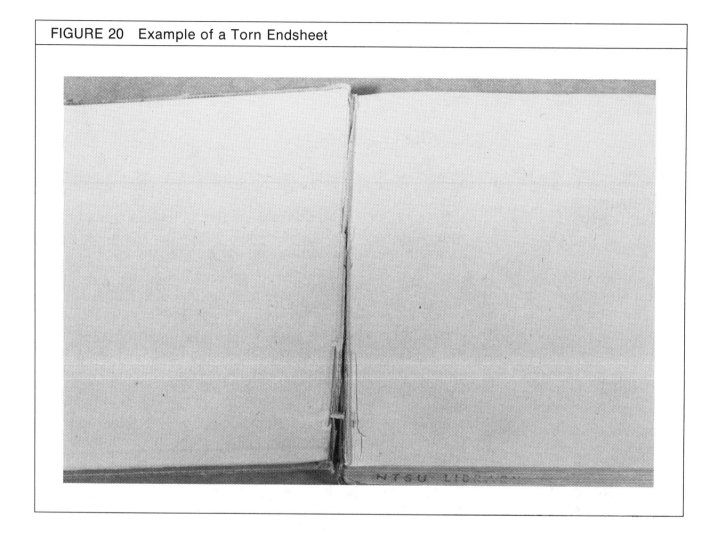

SUPPLIES

Paper for endsheets

PVA

Glue brush

Bone folder

Micro-spatula

Metal ruler and X-Acto® knife or scalpel

Book press or weights

Plywood or other stiff boards

Knitting needles

Wax paper

Waste paper or mylar scraps

Scrap board

OPTIONAL SUPPLIES

Japanese paper

Starch paste

Sandpaper (220 grit)

Nonwoven polyester

PROCEDURE

1. Remove the torn endsheet by gently pulling the tipped-in fly leaf away from the textblock, being careful not to tear the page to which it is attached (see Figure 21a).

2. (Optional) If the original pastedown is partially detached from the board, you can remove it by gently peeling the attached portion of the pastedown away from the board. Then strip off any scraps of endsheet still attached to the board with a micro-spatula (see Figures 21b and c).

3. Lay the book on the table, open one cover, and place enough plywood boards under the open cover to support it.

4. (Optional) Sand the inside of the board to provide a smooth surface for the new endsheet.

5. If the other endsheet needs to be replaced as well, repeat this process. When both boards are ready, continue with step 6 or 7.

6. (Optional) If this book circulates frequently, it is best to strengthen the fold of the endsheets with Japanese paper (a process called *guarding*). This is not necessary, however, for books that circulate infrequently. If extra strength is desired in the endsheet, follow the steps below:

> Tear off a strip of Japanese paper approximately one-inch wide. The tear should be parallel to the chain

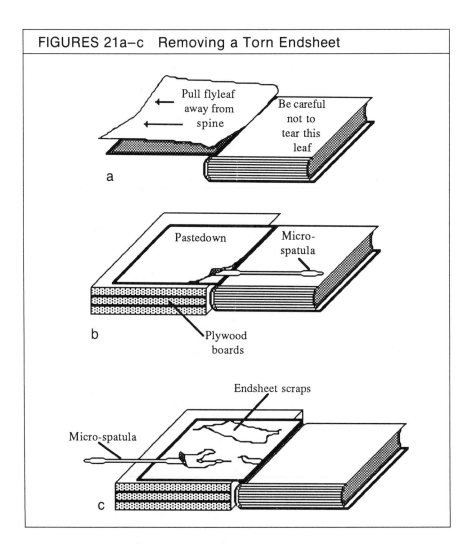

FIGURES 21a–c Removing a Torn Endsheet

a
Pull flyleaf away from spine
Be careful not to tear this leaf

b
Pastedown
Micro-spatula
Plywood boards

c
Endsheet scraps
Micro-spatula

lines of the paper. Methods of tearing Japanese paper are discussed in Chapter 3 under the heading *Japanese Paper and Starch Paste Mends.*

Paste the strip with starch paste, as described below. See Chapter 1 for a paste recipe. Spread paste evenly over a piece of wax paper or polyester film. If less moisture is desired on the mending strip, you can paste out on a piece of blotting paper instead. Lay the mending strip in the paste. Place a piece of waste paper over the mending strip and gently rub the paper with a bone folder to coat the Japanese paper with paste. Remove waste paper and gently lift the mending strip out of the paste using the micro-spatula or tweezers. Do not lift too quickly or the strip will stretch, which will cause the mend to wrinkle as it dries.

- Lay the strip, pasted-side up, on a piece of wax paper or Reemay®. Then place the fold of the endsheet along the center of the strip, tapping the endsheet into place (see Figure 22a).
- Pull the wax paper or Reemay® up and around the fold of the endsheet, pressing gently along the fold. This will fold the strip of Japanese paper around the fold of the endsheet.
- Place the endsheets between sheets of wax paper or

FIGURES 22a–b   Guarding a New Endsheet

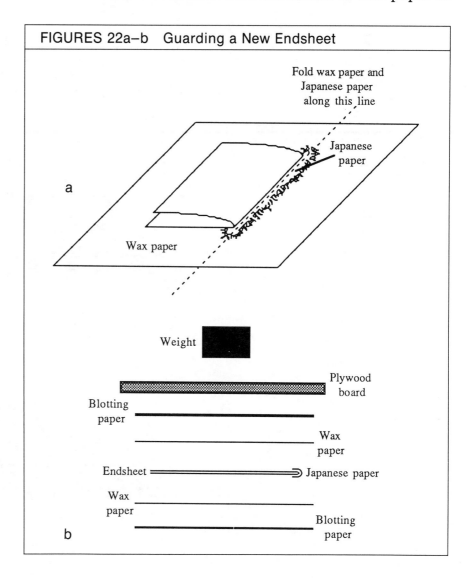

Fold wax paper and Japanese paper along this line

Japanese paper

a

Wax paper

Weight

Plywood board

Blotting paper

Wax paper

Endsheet ⟹ Japanese paper

Wax paper

Blotting paper

b

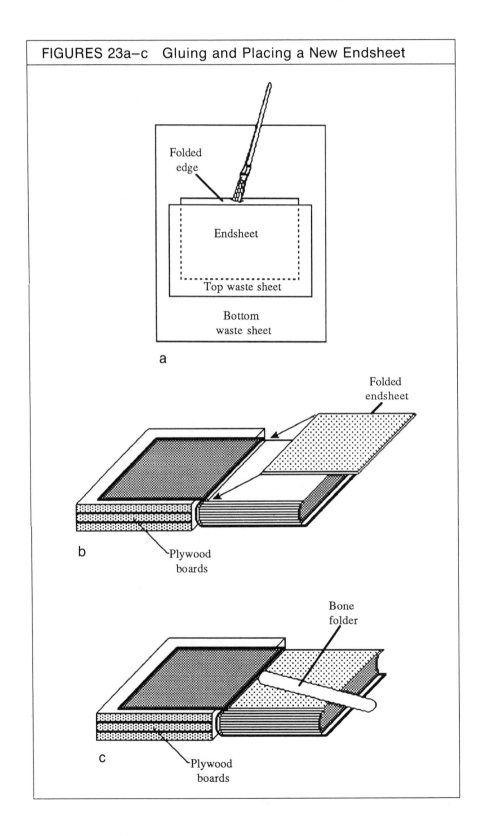

FIGURES 23a–c   Gluing and Placing a New Endsheet

Reemay® and blotting paper. Then place the end-sheets under weights and allow to dry (see Figure 22b).

7. Trim the endsheets to the height of the textblock, using the ruler and knife.

8. Place the endsheet on a piece of waste paper or scrap polyester film. Then place another piece of waste paper on top of the endsheet, leaving approximately ⅛ inch of the folded edge of the endsheet extending beyond the top piece of waste paper. Carefully spread glue along the exposed edge of the endsheet (see Figure 23a).

9. Being careful to align the edges of the endsheet with the edges of the textblock, place the endsheet on the textblock, glued-side down, and gently push the folded edge into the curve of the shoulder with a bone folder (see Figures 23b and c).

10. Close the cover and gently rub the outer hinge with the bone folder.

11. Trim the fore edge of the endsheet to the size of the textblock. To do this, lay the book on the table with the repaired side down. Place a piece of scrap board between the endsheet and the cover. Place the ruler between the endsheet and the textblock, lining up the ruler's edge and the textblock's fore edge. Then cut along the edge of the ruler with the knife (see Figure 24).

12. Turn the book over so that the repaired side is up. Open the cover and support it with plywood boards. Place a piece of waste paper or scrap mylar inside the folded endsheet.

FIGURE 24   Trimming a New Endsheet

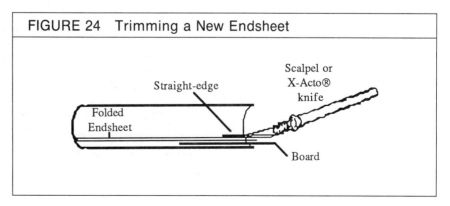

Then, starting in the center of the page near the folded edge, carefully spread glue over the endsheet. Some people prefer to dilute the glue with water for this process. The usual mixture is 3 parts glue to 1 part water (see Figure 25a).

13. Gently lift the glued endsheet just enough to replace the waste paper and make sure the fold of the endsheet is completely down in the hinge of the book. Then lay the endsheet back down and close the cover of the book, pressing gently to adhere the endsheet to the cover. Again, gently rub the outer hinge with the bone folder.

14. Open the cover and remove the waste paper. The endsheet

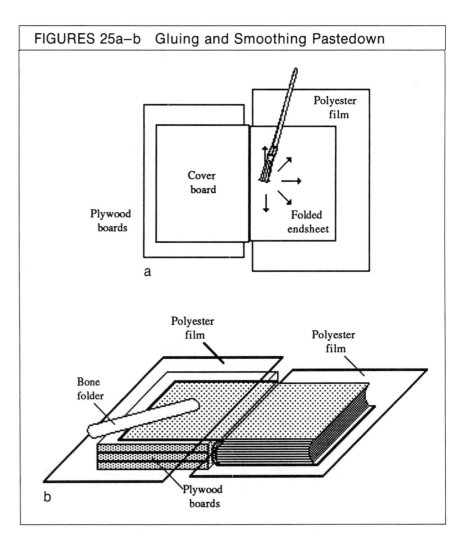

FIGURES 25a–b Gluing and Smoothing Pastedown

should be attached to the board. Supporting the cover with plywood boards, smooth the endsheet by covering it with a fresh piece of waste paper or scrap mylar and rubbing it with the bone folder through this protective layer. When the endsheet is smooth, remove the waste paper or mylar (see Figure 25b).

15. Place wax paper inside the fold of the new endsheet and place the book in a book press or under weights, with a knitting needle in the groove of any outer hinges or joints that have been repaired. This sets the joint.

16. If the other endsheet is being replaced also, repeat steps 6 through 14 for the other endsheet before placing the book under weights.

FIGURE 26   Book with a Torn Spine

REPLACING THE SPINE

When books are given weak or inadequate covering material in the original binding, the piece of material covering the spine can become weakened, if not torn (see Figure 26). This same type of damage can occur because of thoughtless handling, inappropriate shelving, or even from frequent use. This type of damage can be remedied by replacing the original spine with a new spine of bookcloth. Where possible, the bookcloth used for this repair should be of approximately the same weight and color as the original. Publishers, however, have used a wide variety of covering materials, and it is not always feasible, or even possible, to match the original material.

OPTIONAL SUPPLIES

Bristol board or card stock

Cotton cord

SUPPLIES

Bookcloth

Bone folder

PVA and glue brush

Small scissors

Metal ruler and X-Acto® knife or scalpel

Micro-spatula

Cotton or linen cloth

Waste paper or mylar scraps

Wax paper

Weights

Knitting needles

PROCEDURE

1. Remove the original spine piece by cutting along the edges of the spine with the X-Acto® knife or scalpel. Be careful not to cut through the shoulder or the inner hinges of the book. The ruler can be used as a guide for the knife, and the lines of wear will show you where to cut. If the spine is in fairly

good shape, it can be saved, trimmed, and glued back in place on top of the new spine (see Figure 27a).

2. Using the knife or scalpel, slice through the original cover at the top and bottom edge of each board. These slits should be approximately one inch long (see Figure 27b).

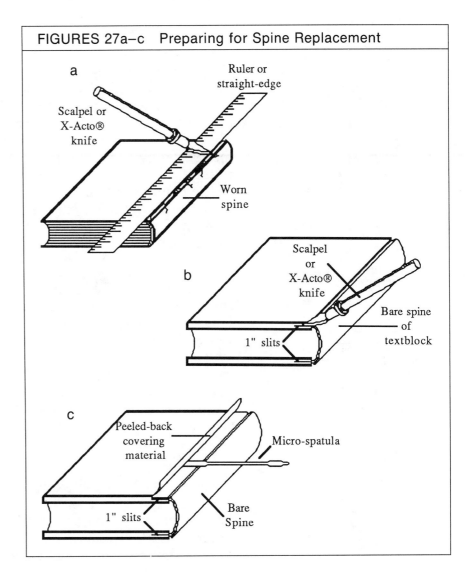

FIGURES 27a–c   Preparing for Spine Replacement

Figures 28a–c

PREPARING A NEW SPINE

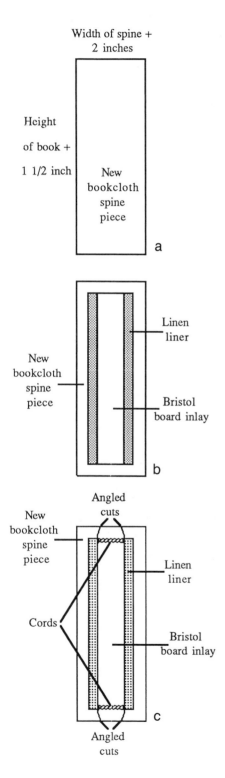

Width of spine + 2 inches

Height of book + 1 1/2 inch — New bookcloth spine piece

a

New bookcloth spine piece — Linen liner / Bristol board inlay

b

New bookcloth spine piece — Angled cuts / Linen liner / Bristol board inlay

Cords

Angled cuts

c

3. Gently peel back the covering material with a micro-spatula, beginning at the spine edge of the board and ending on a line even with the slits made at the top and bottom edges of the boards (see Figure 27c).

4. Cut a piece of bookcloth that is $1\frac{1}{2}$ inches longer than the book is tall and 2 inches wider than the spine of the book. The grain of this piece of bookcloth should be parallel to the spine of the book (see Figure 28a). To measure the spine, wrap a piece of scrap paper around the spine and mark the edges of the spine on this paper. Then measure the distance between the two marks.

5. (Optional) If time, money, and materials allow, it is suggested that you reinforce this piece of bookcloth with an inlay of bristol board or card stock, which can be cut from a stiff manila file folder, and an inner lining of linen or cotton cloth. This is particularly important when reinforcing a book that receives heavy use. The inlay should be exactly the width of the spine and the height of the boards. The linen liner should be the height of the boards, but $\frac{1}{2}$ inch wider than the spine. Glue the linen liner to the center of the bookcloth strip; then glue the inlay to the liner, centered on the bookcloth (see Figure 28b).

6. (Optional) Another refinement of this repair is the addition of small cords to strengthen the head and tail of the new spine. This is accomplished by gluing a piece of cotton string or cord along each end of the inlay. These cords should be exactly as long as the spine inlay is wide. Then make two cuts on each end of the new spine. Begin at the ends of the cords and angle slightly toward the center of the new spine piece as you cut toward the edge of the bookcloth. Spread PVA on the center tabs formed by these cuts and fold these tabs over the cords (see Figure 28c).

7. Spread PVA on the exposed area of the board and place the side flap of the new spine piece on this PVA under the original cover. If you are using the inlay for extra support, be sure that the top and bottom edges of the inlay are lined up with the top and bottom edges of the boards. Use the bone

folder to smooth the new bookcloth into place (see Figures 29a and b).

8. Spread PVA on the underside of the raised original cloth and gently rub it down with the bone folder. It is best to place a piece of waste paper or scrap mylar on the cover and rub through this protective layer (see Figures 29c and d).

9. Repeat steps 7 and 8 for the other side of the new spine.

10. Stand the book on its spine and gently open the boards. Using the X-Acto® knife or scalpel, make two v-shaped cuts in the bookcloth at both the head and tail of the book. Begin the first cut at the hinge and angle slightly toward the center of the spine as you cut toward the edge of the bookcloth. Begin the next cut in the same place as the first and angle slightly toward the board. Remove the small triangle piece. If you used optional steps 5 and 6, you have already made these cuts and folded and glued the center tab before you attached the new spine to the boards (see Figure 30a).

11. Spread PVA on the center tab of the bookcloth and, using the bone folder, tuck it under the spine of the book. Repeat this process for the other end of the book (see Figure 30b).

12. Glue the remaining tabs of bookcloth and fold them over the top and bottom edges of the boards.

13. Place wax paper inside the boards and weight the book between plywood boards or other books. Lay the knitting needles in the grooves of the outer hinges. If you are stacking books on top of each other, place pieces of wax paper between them.

14. If the original spine is still in fairly good condition and if you wish to glue it to the new spine, gently peel off the original lining material and trim any frayed edges. Then spread PVA on the inside of the original spine and place it on the new spine, gently rubbing with a bone folder. It is wise to double check the orientation of the book to be sure you are putting the spine on right-side up.

FIGURES 29a–d   Attaching a New Spine

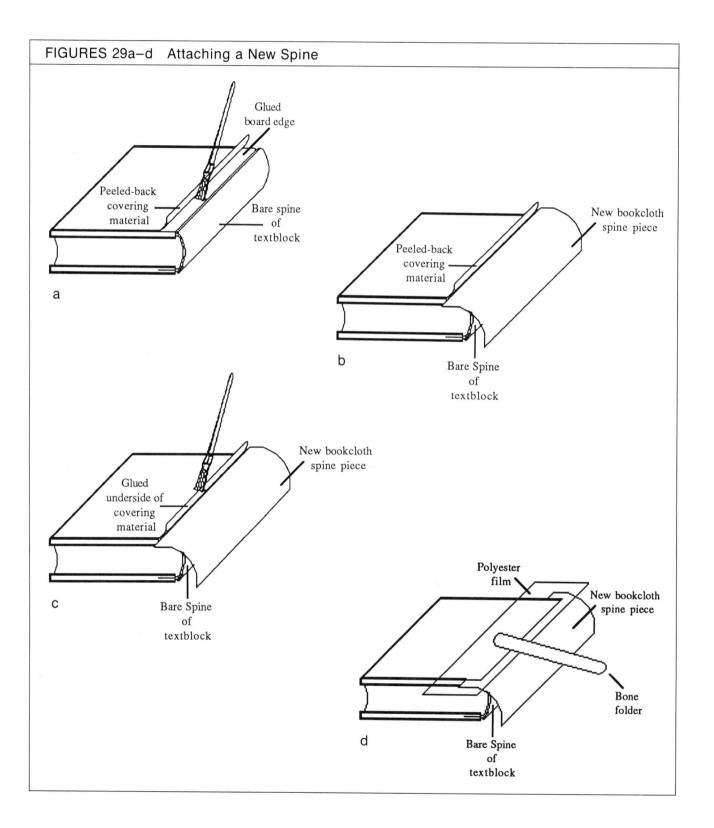

a

Glued
board edge

Peeled-back
covering
material

Bare spine
of
textblock

b

Peeled-back
covering
material

New bookcloth
spine piece

Bare Spine
of
textblock

c

Glued
underside of
covering
material

New bookcloth
spine piece

Bare Spine
of
textblock

d

Polyester
film

New bookcloth
spine piece

Bone
folder

Bare Spine
of
textblock

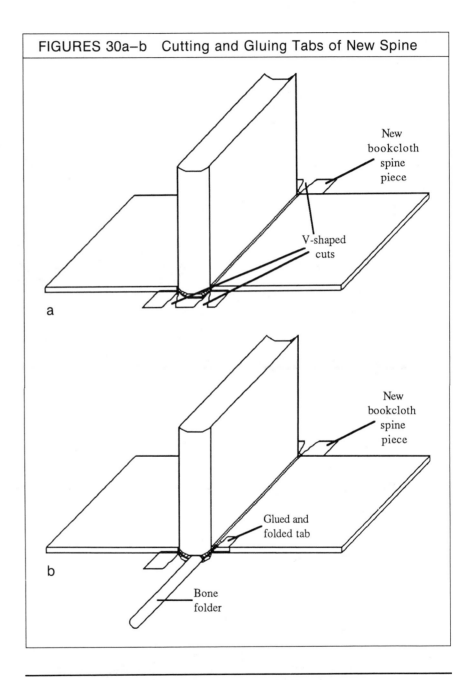

FIGURES 30a–b   Cutting and Gluing Tabs of New Spine

New
bookcloth
spine
piece

V-shaped
cuts

a

New
bookcloth
spine
piece

Glued and
folded tab

b

Bone
folder

REPLACING ONE INNER HINGE

Sometimes, one or both hinges of a book have become completely separated from the textblock, or nearly so (see Figure 31). If the book has only one torn hinge, and if the case is still intact, the following procedure is recommended. If both

FIGURE 31 Weakened Inner Hinge

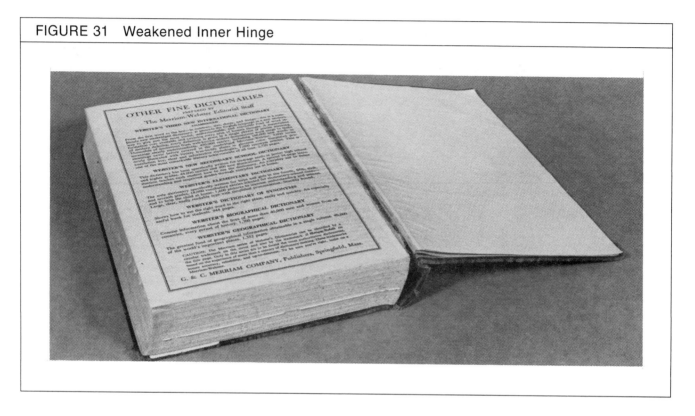

hinges are torn, it is recommended that you recase the book (discussed later in this chapter).

OPTIONAL SUPPLIES

Dissecting needle or ice pick

Linen thread

Large sewing needles such as doll needles

Beeswax

SUPPLIES

Cloth

PVA and glue brush

Metal ruler and X-Acto® knife or scalpel

Scissors

Wax paper

Waste paper or scrap mylar

Plywood or other stiff boards

Weights

PROCEDURE

1. Carefully cut through whatever is left of the broken hinge, avoiding the cloth of the outer case (see Figure 32a). If the book was sewn on tapes, cut them off at the edge of the spine.

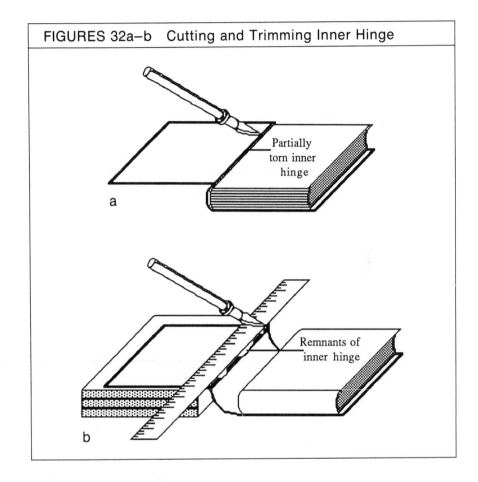

FIGURES 32a–b   Cutting and Trimming Inner Hinge

Partially torn inner hinge

a

Remnants of inner hinge

b

2. Support the loose cover with plywood or other stiff boards and trim any excess material on the spine edge of the boards and on the edge of the spine. (See Figure 32b.)

3. Cut a piece of cotton or linen cloth that is $\frac{1}{8}$ inch shorter than the textblock and 1 inch to $1\frac{1}{2}$ inches wide. This cloth will form the new hinge (see Figure 33a).

4. Place the cloth on a piece of waste paper and another piece of waste paper on top of the cloth. One long edge of the cloth should extend $\frac{1}{8}$ inch beyond the top piece of waste paper. Then spread PVA on the exposed $\frac{1}{8}$-inch strip (see Figure 33b).

5. Place the glued edge of the cloth, glued side down, along the shoulder of the textblock (see Figure 33c). Using a bone

Figures 33a–c

GLUING AND ATTACHING NEW INNER HINGE

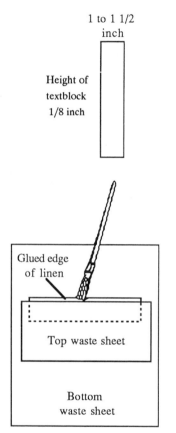

1 to 1 1/2 inch

Height of textblock 1/8 inch

Glued edge of linen

Top waste sheet

Bottom waste sheet

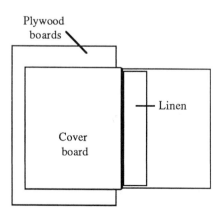

Plywood boards

Linen

Cover board

folder, gently rub the glued section of cloth into place in the shoulder of the book. If you do not intend to use the optional steps 6 and 7, be sure to allow the PVA to dry thoroughly before continuing.

6. (Optional) If the book is particularly thick or heavy, it is best to sew the cloth to the textblock in addition to gluing. To do this, place five marks on the spine where you will punch holes for the sewing. These holes should begin $\frac{1}{2}$ inch from the head or tail and proceed at approximately $1\frac{1}{2}$-inch intervals, ending $\frac{1}{2}$ inch from the opposite end. On tall books, more than five holes may be needed. This is acceptable, but be sure to mark out an odd number of holes and not to allow the holes to be closer together than one inch.

7. (Optional) Using the dissecting needle or ice pick, punch holes at the marks made in step 6. You should gently push the dissecting needle from the inside of the shoulder, coming out through the spine. The angle of these holes should alternate; begin with a shallow-angled hole and continue with first a more deeply angled hole, then another shallow hole (see Figures 34a and b).

8. (Optional) Cut a piece of linen thread three times the length of the book, and thread one end of it through a sewing needle. Wax the thread with beeswax and thread the other end through a needle as well. Put one needle through the first hole at one end of the textblock and draw it through until equal lengths of thread extend on each side, as if beginning to lace a shoe. Take the needle on the shoulder side of the hole and put it through the second hole from the shoulder side. Take the other needle (on the spine side) and put it through the second hole from the spine side. Continue to lace the thread through the holes until you come to the last hole. On the final hole, run only the shoulder-side thread through the hole. Using a square knot, tie the two ends of the thread together near the second hole from the end and shift the knot into this hole (see Figures 34c and d).

9. Cut the loose corners from the cloth so that the edges angle toward the center of the textblock (see Figure 35a).

10. Slice through the turn-ins at the head and tail of the spine

edge of the board. These cuts should be as long as the linen is wide. Then gently peel up the pastedown, beginning at the spine edge and continuing until the end of the cuts are reached (see Figures 35b and c).

11. Place a piece of waste paper or scrap polyester film between the new hinge and the textblock. Then spread PVA on the exposed side of the linen, starting in the center toward the spine and working outward (see Figure 36a).

12. Lift the board up enough to position the linen hinge between the board and pastedown, stretching the linen tightly across the newly formed hinge (see Figure 36b). Rub the linen with the bone folder to remove any creases; then close the book and rub the outer hinge lightly with the bone folder.

13. Open the book again and spread PVA on the underside of the lifted portion of the endsheet (see Figure 36c). Then

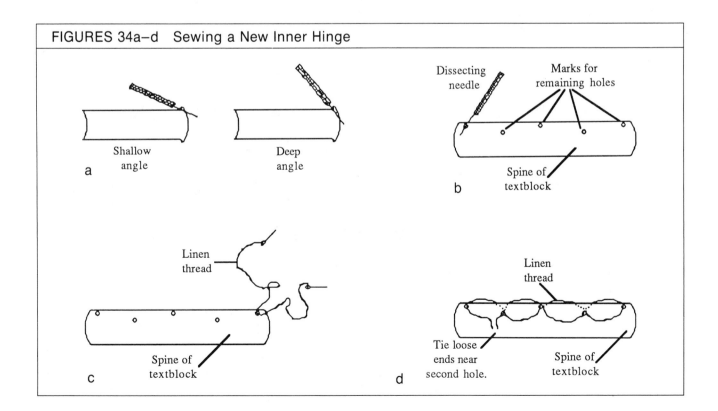

FIGURES 34a–d   Sewing a New Inner Hinge

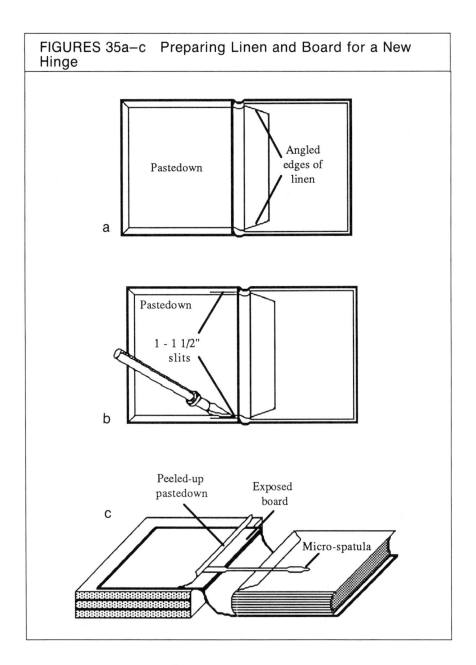

FIGURES 35a–c   Preparing Linen and Board for a New Hinge

a

Pastedown

Angled edges of linen

b

Pastedown

1 - 1 1/2" slits

c

Peeled-up pastedown

Exposed board

Micro-spatula

lay the endsheet back into place and rub down with a bone folder through a piece of waste paper or mylar.

14. Place a piece of wax paper between the board and the fly leaf. Close the book, lay the knitting needles in the grooves of the outer hinges, and allow the PVA to dry under boards and weights.

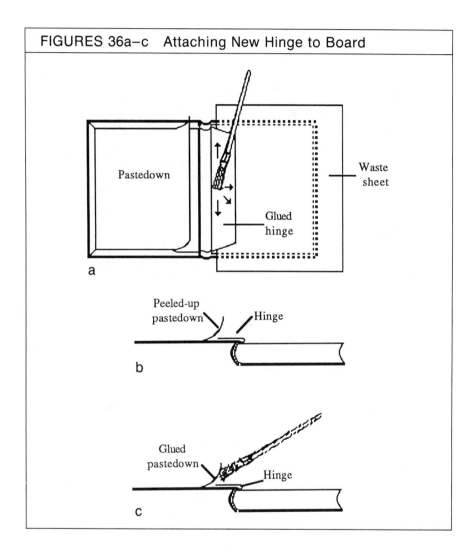

FIGURES 36a–c Attaching New Hinge to Board

RECASING THE TEXTBLOCK

Damage to the spine and hinges can become particularly severe when it is coupled with torn endsheets. In the worst cases, the textblock becomes completely separated from the case (see Figure 37). This type of damage can be repaired only by recasing the textblock. In many cases, the original case can be reattached to the textblock. Recasing actually involves more than one procedure. For example, you will need to replace the endsheets (described earlier in this chapter) when you recase a book. You can also strengthen the hinges of the

FIGURE 37   Textblock Completely Separated from Case

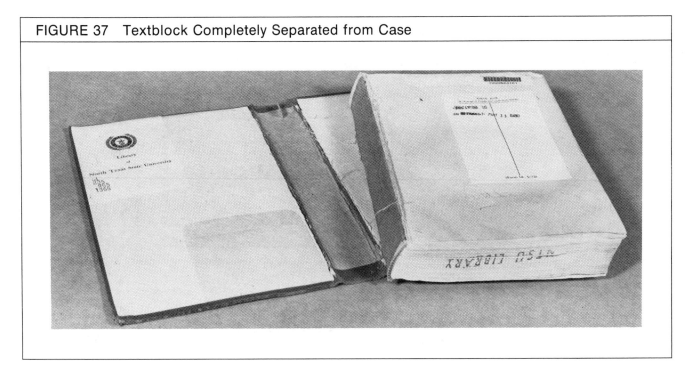

original case by lining the spine (described in the following section) in preparation for recasing.

SUPPLIES

Bookcloth

Endsheets

Bone folder

PVA and glue brush

Small scissors

Metal ruler and X-Acto® knife or scalpel

Linen or cotton cloth

Bristol board or card stock

Waste paper or scraps of polyester film

Wax paper

Sand paper (220 grit)

Plywood or other stiff boards

Weights

Knitting needles

OPTIONAL SUPPLIES

Japanese paper

Starch paste

PROCEDURE

1. Remove the cover from the textblock, without cutting the cloth of the outer hinge. This may involve carefully cutting through partially torn endsheets, super, and remnants of tapes if the book was sewn on tapes. You may also have to remove the fly leaf side of the original endsheet (see Figures 38a and b).

2. The spine of the textblock must be cleaned before the book can be recased. Any loose material from the original paper lining should be removed. This can be done by simply pulling off the loose parts or gently scraping the spine with the dull, or back, edge of a knife. The cloth super and original glue can be left intact unless they are severely deteriorated. In such a case, it is best to turn the book over to a conservator.

3. (Optional) If this book circulates frequently, it is best to

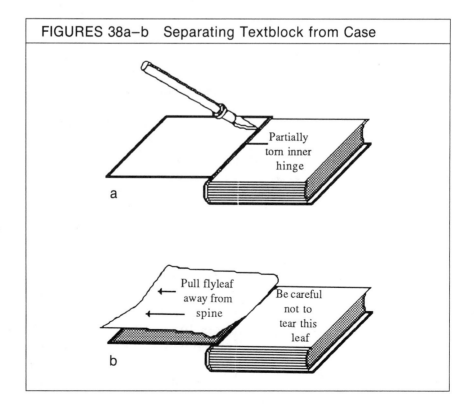

FIGURES 38a–b Separating Textblock from Case

Partially torn inner hinge

a

Pull flyleaf away from spine

Be careful not to tear this leaf

b

strengthen the fold of the new endsheets with Japanese paper, a process called *guarding*. This is not necessary, however, for books that circulate infrequently. If extra strength is desired in the endsheet, follow the steps below.

- Tear off a strip of Japanese paper approximately 1-inch wide. The tear should be parallel to the chain lines of the paper. Methods of tearing Japanese paper are discussed in Chapter 3 under the heading "Japanese Paper and Starch Paste Mends."
- Paste the strip with starch paste, as described below. (See Chapter 1 for a paste recipe.) Spread paste evenly over a piece of wax paper or polyester film. If less moisture is desired on the mending strip, you can paste out on a piece of blotting paper instead. Lay the mending strip in the paste. Place a piece of waste paper over the mending strip and gently rub the paper with a bone folder to coat the Japanese paper with paste. Remove waste paper and gently lift the mending strip out of the paste using the micro-spatula or tweezers. Do not lift too quickly or the strip will stretch, which will cause the mend to wrinkle as it dries.
- Lay the strip, pasted-side up, on a piece of wax paper or Reemay®. Then place the fold of the endsheet along the center of the strip, tapping the endsheet into place (see Figure 39a).
- Pull the wax paper or Reemay® up and around the fold of the endsheet, pressing gently along the fold. This will fold the strip of Japanese paper around the fold of the endsheet.
- Place the endsheets between sheets of wax paper or Reemay®and blotting paper. Then place the endsheets under weights and allow to dry (see Figure 39b).

4. Trim the new endsheets to the height of the textblock. On a piece of waste paper, glue a ⅛-inch strip along the spine edge of the folded endsheet, using another piece of waste paper to cover the rest of the endsheet. Then carefully place the endsheet on the textblock, glued-side down, and gently push the folded edge into the curve of the shoulder with a bone folder.

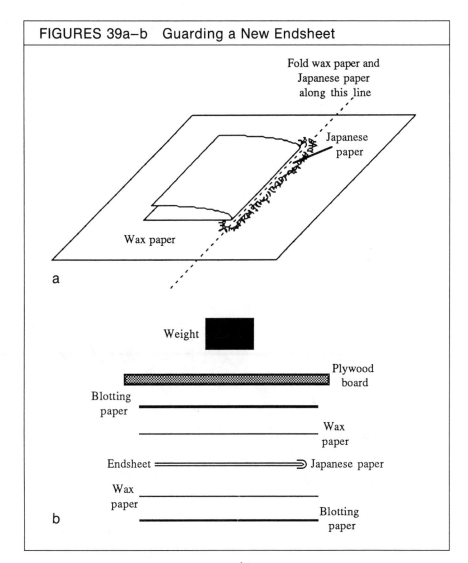

FIGURES 39a–b   Guarding a New Endsheet

Fold wax paper and
Japanese paper
along this line

Japanese
paper

Wax paper

a

Weight

Plywood
board

Blotting
paper

Wax
paper

Endsheet ===========⇒ Japanese paper

Wax
paper

Blotting
paper

b

5. Cut a piece of paper that is ⅛ inch shorter than the spine and as wide as the spine. This paper can be brown kraft paper or leftover endsheet paper; the grain should run parallel to the spine.

6. Spread PVA on the spine of the textblock and position the paper on the spine (see Figure 40a). Rub it down with the bone folder. Then set the textblock aside while you prepare the case.

7. Cut a piece of cotton or linen cloth that is ¼ inch shorter than the spine and 2-inches wider than the spine. This piece

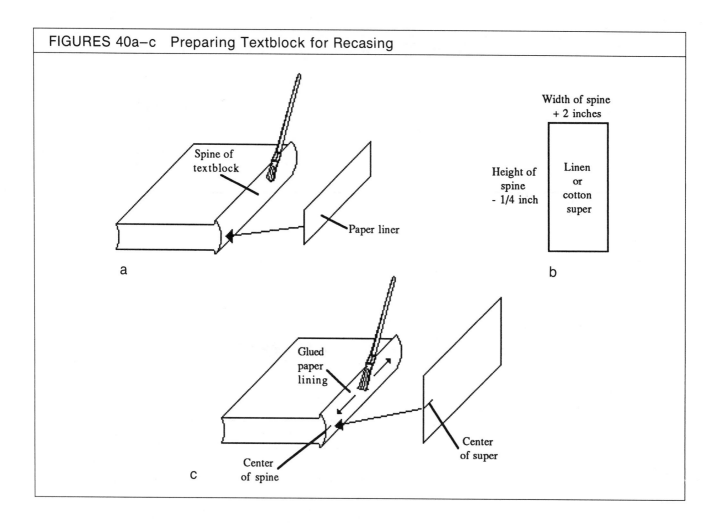

FIGURES 40a–c   Preparing Textblock for Recasing

a — Spine of textblock — Paper liner

b — Width of spine + 2 inches — Height of spine - 1/4 inch — Linen or cotton super

c — Glued paper lining — Center of spine — Center of super

of cloth will be the new super and will form the hinges that will hold the textblock to the case (see Figure 40b).

8. Spread PVA on the spine of the textblock and center the new super on the spine with approximately one inch of the super extending past either side of the spine (see Figure 40c). Rub the super into place with the bone folder.

9. Remove the old super from the boards and trim off any excess paper on the spine edge of the boards (see Figure 41a). This will tear the original pastedown, the remnants of which can be left in place. If the original pastedown was not well attached to the board, it can be gently peeled off (see Figure 41b). If the super has left a rough surface on the boards, they should be sanded lightly.

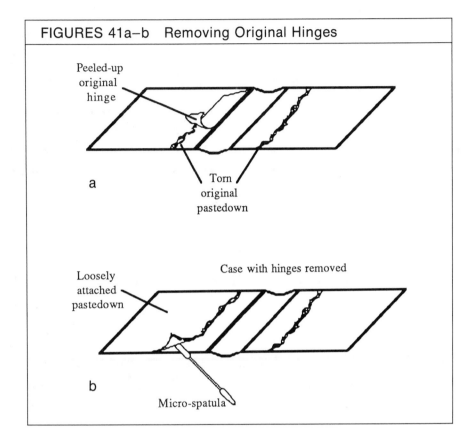

FIGURES 41a–b   Removing Original Hinges

Peeled-up original hinge

a

Torn original pastedown

Loosely attached pastedown

Case with hinges removed

b

Micro-spatula

10. (Optional) If the cloth of the case is particularly worn or even torn in the hinge area, you can line the spine with book-cloth. This process is described in steps 10 through 16. If you choose to add this procedure, you must follow all of the steps. To begin this process, you will have to slice through the turn-ins one inch from the spine edge of the boards and gently peel up the flaps made by these cuts. Carefully peel away the orig-inal inlay from the spine (see Figure 42a).

11. (Optional) You will also have to peel the original cloth away from the boards, beginning at the spine edge and ending on a line even with the cuts made in the turn-ins (see Figure 42b).

12. (Optional) Cut a piece of bookcloth that is 2-inches wider than the spine and 2-inches longer than the boards. Carefully spread a thin layer of PVA on the inside of the original spine and adjacent areas of cloth that were peeled

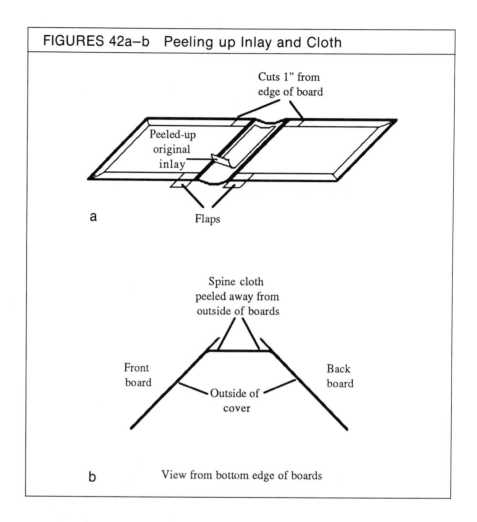

FIGURES 42a–b   Peeling up Inlay and Cloth

Cuts 1" from edge of board

Peeled-up original inlay

a

Flaps

Spine cloth peeled away from outside of boards

Front board

Back board

Outside of cover

b   View from bottom edge of boards

up from the boards (see Figure 43a). If the cloth of the original cover is particularly worn or fragile in the spine area, you should spread the PVA on the new bookcloth lining instead. To glue the bookcloth, lay it face up on the table with a piece of waste paper covering $1\frac{1}{4}$ inches of the bookcloth at each end. Weight the waste paper and spread PVA on the exposed portion of the bookcloth.

13. (Optional) Place one edge of the new bookcloth lining between one board and the glued cloth. The face of the bookcloth should be against the PVA. Continue to lay the lining onto the PVA and place the other edge under the other board. The new lining should extend approximately one inch beyond the head and tail of the case. Lay the case flat and rub the lining down with the bone folder. Then turn the case over,

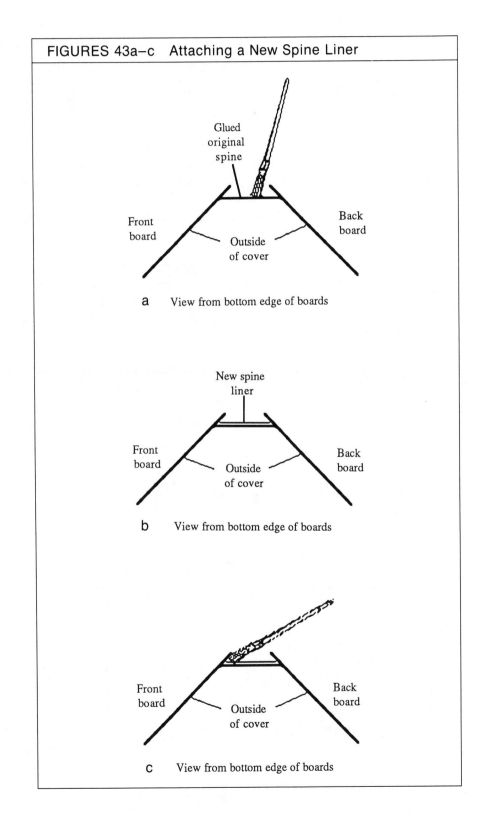

FIGURES 43a–c Attaching a New Spine Liner

a View from bottom edge of boards

b View from bottom edge of boards

c View from bottom edge of boards

smooth out any loose material, and remove any excess PVA with a fingertip. If you glued the new bookcloth instead of the original case, spread a small amount of PVA under the top and bottom of the original spine piece of the case and rub them down (see Figure 43b).

14. (Optional) Turn the case back over so that the inside of the case is facing up and spread PVA on the boards where the original cloth was peeled away (see Figure 43c). Press the boards down onto the liner and rub with a bone folder. Turn the case over again and rub the cloth down on the glued area of the boards.

15. (Optional) Cut an inlay of bristol board or other card stock that is as long as the boards and exactly as wide as the spine. Glue the inlay and place it in the center of the inside of the new spine lining (see Figure 44a). Rub the inlay with the bone folder.

16. (Optional) Trim the ends of the lining so that they are even with the original turn-ins. You may want to glue a piece of cotton string or cord along each end of the inlay to strengthen the folds at the head and tail of the lining. These cords should be exactly as long as the spine inlay is wide.

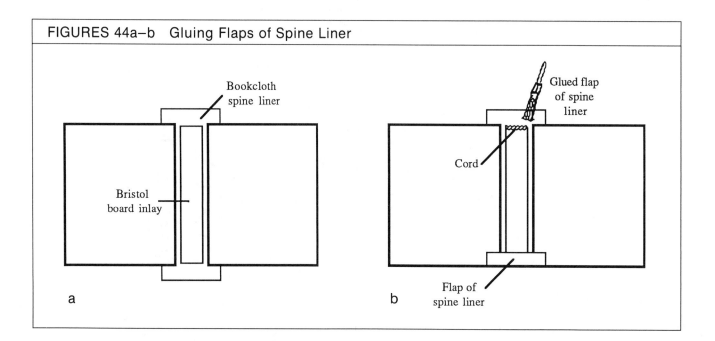

FIGURES 44a–b   Gluing Flaps of Spine Liner

Spread PVA on the ends of the lining. Then fold these tabs, the new turn-ins, over the ends of the inlay and board edges (see Figure 44b). Rub them down with the bone folder.

17. With the case open, place the textblock on the back board. Be sure to put the textblock in right-side up. Check the fit of

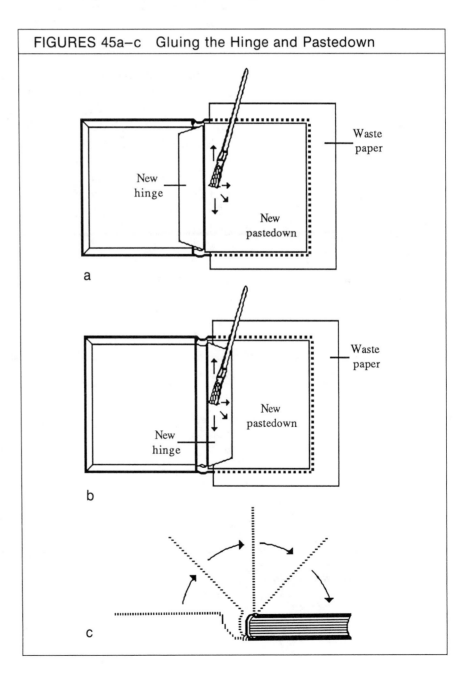

FIGURES 45a–c   Gluing the Hinge and Pastedown

the case by folding the spine and front board around the textblock. If the spine of the textblock is curved, you may need to shape the spine of the case by gently bending it around a pipe or broom handle.

18. Place a piece of waste paper under the new pastedown and spread PVA between the hinge and pastedown. Rub the hinge down on the pastedown and glue out the hinge and the rest of the pastedown (see Figures 45a and b).

19. Remove the waste paper and carefully close the cover, bringing the spine of the cover up against the spine of the textblock and then laying the board down on the glued hinge and pastedown (see Figure 45c). Rub down the outer hinges with the bone folder.

20. Lift the textblock so that it is standing on its spine and gently open the cover you have just glued into place. Cover the pastedown with scrap polyester film and rub it carefully with a bone folder to remove any bubbles or wrinkles (see Figure 46a).

21. Repeat steps 18, 19, and 20 for the back cover.

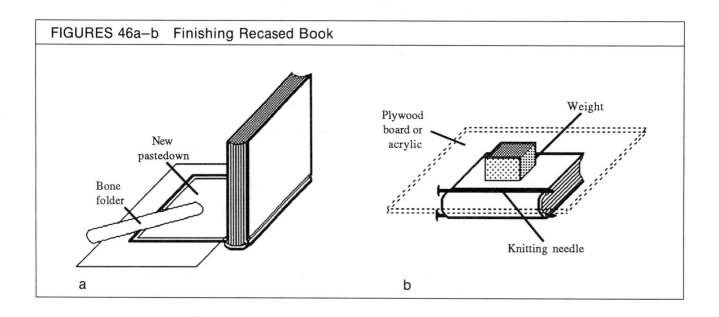

FIGURES 46a–b   Finishing Recased Book

New pastedown

Bone folder

Plywood board or acrylic

Weight

Knitting needle

a

b

22. Place wax paper inside the boards and weight the book under a plywood board or other books. Lay knitting needles in the grooves of the outer hinges (see Figure 46b). If you are stacking books on top of each other, place pieces of wax paper between them. Allow the PVA to dry.

SECTION 2: PAPERBOUND BOOKS

Paperback books present a rather difficult problem. They are the least expensive type of book, but also the least durable with inherently weak spines and hinges. While their price makes them very desirable, their instability makes them very difficult to keep for any length of time. There are, however, a number of ways to strengthen the hinges and spines of paperback books without adding too much to their overall cost. Most library vendors offer several products for strengthening paperbacks. The simplest is book tape, which can be applied to the spine of a paperback. Pressure sensitive laminate films are also offered for the protection of the covers as well as the spines of paperbacks. These are usually available in pre-cut sizes or in rolls and in a variety of weights. Some companies also offer clear, nonadhesive, adjustable covers that can be reused.

If you opt for one of the commercially available methods of strengthening paperbacks, it is suggested that you use one of the laminates that allows a portion of the film to fold over the edges of the cover like the turn-ins on a clothbound book. These laminates protect the edges of the paper cover as well as its outer surface. The heavier, rigid laminates should only be used on books that will not be kept for a great length of time, since these covers can ultimately pull the cover away from the textblock. The exceptions are laminates that are rigid over the covers, but are flexible where they wrap around the spine. These covers can be very useful and are less likely to pull the cover away from the textblock.

Paperback books can also be reinforced with cloth hinges and boards. There are various methods of performing this procedure, which differ in the weight of the boards used and in the treatment of the cover. Some methods retain the original cover, and others hide or replace it. Two methods are discussed in the following section.

REINFORCING PAPERBACK SPINES WITH BOOK TAPE

The spine of a paperback book can be reinforced simply by applying book tape to the spine and allowing it to extend onto the covers. This procedure can also be used to reattach covers that have been torn off at the spine.

SUPPLIES

Book tape

Ruler

Scissors

Bone folder

PROCEDURE

1. Place the paperback on the table with the spine of the book extending slightly beyond the edge of the table.

2. Select a roll of book tape that is $1\frac{1}{2}$ to 2 inches wider than the spine of the book. Cut a piece from this roll that is $1\frac{1}{2}$ to 2 inches longer than the book is tall.

3. Center the tape on the spine of the book and gently press the tape into place (see Figure 47a).

4. (Optional) If you are reattaching a front or back cover, position the cover on the textblock, lining up the fore edge, top, and bottom of the cover with the fore edge, top, and bottom of the textblock. Then fold the flap of tape over the cover and press into place. Rub the tape firmly with the bone folder.

5. Stand the book on its spine and gently lay it down on first one flap of tape, then the other. Using the bone folder, rub the tape firmly into place on the spine and the front and back covers of the book (see Figures 47b and c).

6. Using the scissors, make small cuts in the flaps of tape at the head and tail of the spine. These cuts should be in a line with the corners of the spine (see Figure 47d).

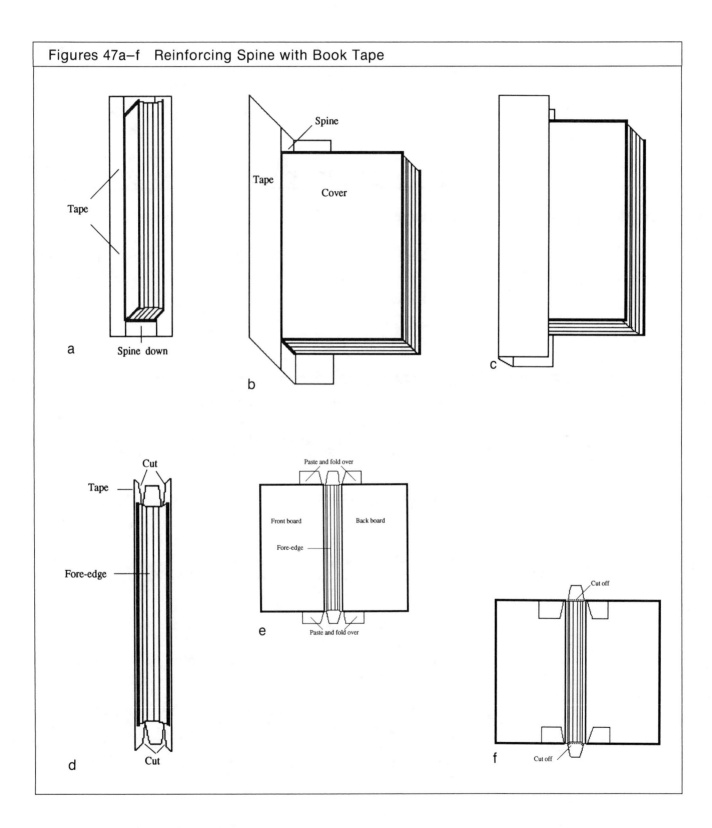

Figures 47a–f   Reinforcing Spine with Book Tape

7. Open one cover and fold over the outer flaps formed by the cuts. Press the tape firmly into place. Repeat for the other cover. Then cut off the remaining center flap of tape at the head and tail of the spine (see Figures 47e and f).

LAMINATING PAPERBACK BOOKS

OPTIONAL SUPPLIES

Measuring grid

SUPPLIES

Repositionable laminating film (in pre-cut paperback sizes or in a roll)

Ruler

Scissors

Bone folder

PROCEDURE

1. Cut a piece of laminating film that is 2 inches longer than the book is tall and 2 inches wider than twice the width of the book plus the depth of the book. If you are using pre-cut laminating film, choose a cover that is the appropriate size for the book you are reinforcing.

2. Peel the backing from the laminate and lay it on the table adhesive side up. You may want to place a measuring grid under the laminate to assist in centering the book on the film. If you are using pre-cut laminating film, follow the manufacturer's instructions as to which portion of the laminate should be uncovered and adhered first.

3. Center the closed book on one end of the laminate, with one inch of film extending beyond the head, tail, and fore edge of the book. Press the book gently onto the laminating film (see Figure 48a).

4. Fold the laminating film up around the spine, pressing out any bubbles on the spine. Continue wrapping the film around the other cover of the book, pressing out any bubbles that form on the cover (see Figure 48b). Then rub both covers and the spine with a bone folder.

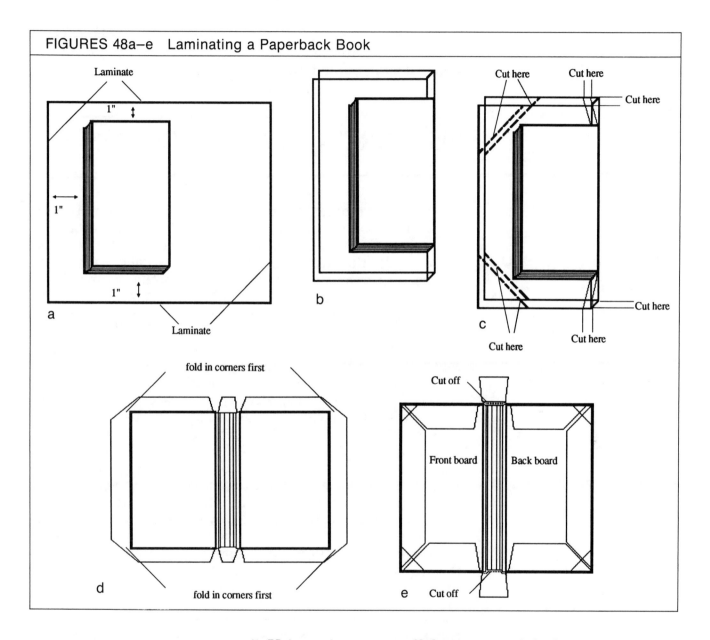

FIGURES 48a–e   Laminating a Paperback Book

5. Using scissors, cut off the corners of the laminate at a 45-degree angle, $\frac{1}{16}$ inch to $\frac{1}{8}$ inch from the corner of the paper cover. Then make two angled cuts in the laminating film even with the corners of the spine at the head and tail (see Figure 48c).

6. Open the book and fold in the angled corners. Then fold the flaps of film around the fore edge, top, and bottom of each

cover, rubbing them firmly into place with a bone folder. Then cut off the remaining tabs of film at the head and tail of the spine (see Figure 48d and e).

REINFORCING PAPERBACKS WITH BOARDS

The covers and spines of paperbacks may also be strengthened using cloth and a thin board. There are various methods of adding boards to a paperback book. Of the two methods discussed here, the first reinforces the paperback with inner hinges, utilizes a thinner board, and allows the original cover to show. The second method reinforces the paperback with outer hinges, utilizes a thicker board, and hides the original cover, which is retained but is no longer visible without lifting the new outer cover. These two procedures will be discussed separately.

These procedures provide a stronger cover for the book, whereas the use of tape, already discussed, serves only to protect the original cover. Large format paperbacks or paperback reference books are good candidates for reinforcement with boards. Perfect-bound paperbacks are best preserved by adding inner hinges, as the addition of outer hinges and heavier boards can cause the cover to separate from the textblock. The addition of inner hinges is also the best alternative when it is important that the original cover remain visible, which may be the case with art books. Reference books might best be preserved by adding outer hinges and heavier boards since they are used so frequently.

REINFORCING PAPERBACKS WITH INNER HINGES

SUPPLIES

Bristol board (.010 inch or .030 inch)

Linen or cotton cloth

PVA

Glue brush

Scissors

Metal ruler and X-Acto® knife or scalpel

Bone folder

Weights and plywood boards

Waste paper or scraps of polyester film

Wax paper

PROCEDURE

1. Cut two pieces of Bristol board that are precisely the height of the book and ¼ inch narrower than the book is wide. The grain of these boards should run parallel to the spine of the book.

2. Cut two pieces of cloth that are the height of the book and 1 inch wide.

3. If the cover is tipped onto the first and last leaves of the book, carefully separate the cover from the inner edge of these leaves. Do not separate the cover from the spine, just from the first and last leaves (see Figure 49a).

4. Open the book, spread PVA evenly on one piece of cloth. Position this piece of cloth along the inner hinge of one cover. Half of the cloth strip should rest on the cover and half on the first leaf of the textblock. Use the bone folder to rub the cloth tightly into place (see Figure 49b).

5. Spread PVA evenly on a piece of Bristol board and place it on the inside of the cover, aligning the fore edge, top, and bottom of the board with the fore edge, top, and bottom of the original cover (see Figures 49c and d).

6. Place a piece of wax paper between the cover and first page, close the book, and rub the cover with a bone folder over a piece of polyester film.

FIGURES 49a–d   Reinforcing with Inner Hinges

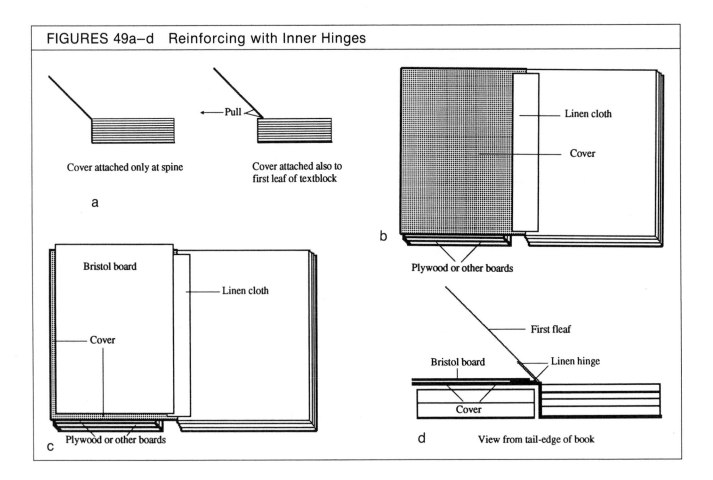

Cover attached only at spine

←—Pull

Cover attached also to
first leaf of textblock

a

Linen cloth

Cover

b

Plywood or other boards

Bristol board

Linen cloth

Cover

Plywood or other boards

c

First fleaf

Bristol board

Linen hinge

Cover

d   View from tail-edge of book

7. Turn the book over and repeat steps 4 through 6 for the back cover of the book.

8. Allow the PVA to dry overnight under weights.

REINFORCING PAPERBACKS WITH OUTER HINGES

SUPPLIES

Pressboard or barrier board (up to .060 inch)

Linen or cotton cloth

Figures 50a–c

ATTACHING BOARDS

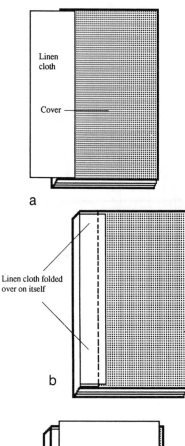

Linen cloth

Cover

a

Linen cloth folded over on itself

b

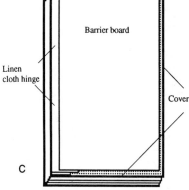

Barrier board

Linen cloth hinge

Cover

c

Bookcloth

PVA

Glue brush

Scissors

Metal ruler and X-Acto® knife or scalpel

Bone folder

Weights and plywood boards

Sandpaper (220 grit)

Waste paper or scraps of polyester film

Wax paper

PROCEDURE

1. Cut two pieces of board that are as long as the book is tall and ¼ inch narrower than the book is wide.

2. Cut two pieces of cloth to the height of the book and 1 inch wide.

3. Cut one piece of bookcloth that is 2 inches wider than the spine of the book and 2 inches longer than the height of the book.

4. (Optional) If you are covering a paperback with a shiny or glossy cover, you can lightly sand a ½-inch strip along the spine edge of the front and back covers. This will allow the PVA to adhere better to the cover.

5. Spread PVA evenly on one of the small pieces of cloth and place it along the spine edge of the front cover. Approximately ⅜ inch to ½ inch of the cloth should be attached to the cover; the rest should extend beyond the spine (see Figure 50a).

6. Fold the cloth back over itself on a line even with the spine, leaving the unattached portion of the glued side facing up (see Figure 50b).

7. Place a board on the glued cloth, aligning the fore edge, top, and bottom of the board with the fore edge, top, and bottom of the original cover (see Figure 50c).

8. Repeat steps 5 through 7 for the back cover of the book.

9. Spread PVA on the spine of the book and position it in the center of the large piece of bookcloth.

10. Make two cuts in the tabs of bookcloth that extend beyond

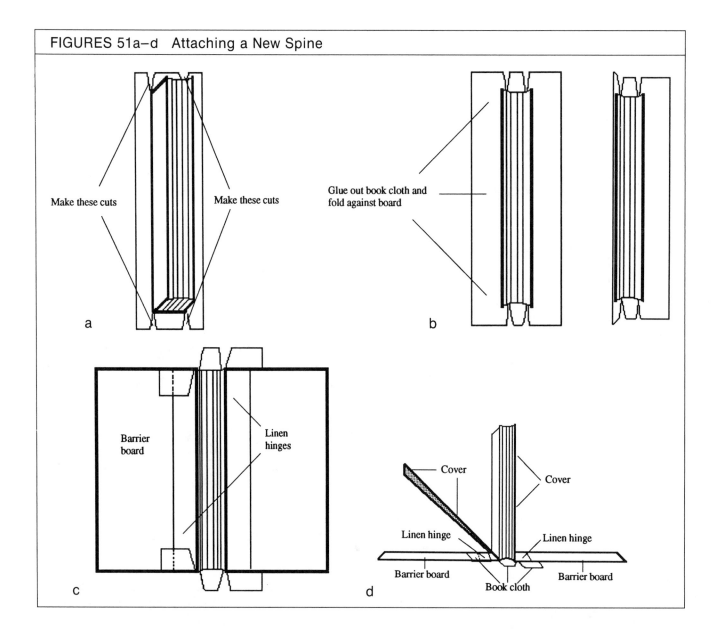

FIGURES 51a–d   Attaching a New Spine

the head and tail of the book. These cuts should be on a line with the corners of the spine (see Figure 51a).

11. Spread PVA on one side flap of bookcloth and turn the flap over onto the cover. Lift the board and fold the tabs at head and tail over the inside of the board. Repeat this process for the other side flap and trim the remaining flap at head and tail so that it is even with the top and bottom of the spine (see Figures 51b through e).

12. Put wax paper between the original cover and the new boards; allow the PVA to dry under weights.

ALTERNATIVE CONSERVATION SUGGESTIONS

All of the procedures discussed in this chapter will extend the life of a book, but they are not permanent. For example, if you tighten the hinges of a casebound book that receives heavy use, its hinges will eventually begin to give way again. Even laminating films, which will probably outlast the paper of a paperback book, will not ensure that the textblock and the cover do not separate. It is important to note that none of these procedures are archivally sound because they cannot be reversed without causing harm to the object. If you have books that require a more permanent solution to hinge and spine problems it is best to have them rebound. Rebinding should be left to a commercial bindery, preferably a bindery that is capable of library binding. Such binderies will be associated with the Library Binding Institute. If you have books of greater artistic, bibliographic, or historic value, they should receive full conservation treatment. If this treatment is not within your budget, a protective enclosure should be made for such items. Some of the enclosures discussed in Chapter 5 might be considered as alternative procedures for these books. They might also be considered for books that have damage to the hinges or spine but do not circulate very often. For example, a casebound book that has loose hinges can be given a book wrap if it does not receive much use.

FURTHER READINGS

Repairs for Casebound Books:

 Greenfield, pp. 129–156.

 Kyle, pp. 77–94.

 Morrow, pp. 15–80.

Repairs for Paperbound Books:

 Greenfield, pp. 156–158.

 Morrow, pp. 93–104.

5 PROTECTIVE ENCLOSURES

Many books in your library are probably in such a deteriorated state that the covers either have separated from the textblock or are about to. You may also have several odd sizes of AV materials, or large flat objects like posters or maps. You may even have photo albums or videotapes. All of these items are candidates for protective enclosures. Enclosures can serve two purposes—to hold together an item with several parts, whether a book with loose boards or a filmstrip and its accompanying audiotape; and to protect special items, such as books with designer bindings.

Many types of enclosures are commercially available, including mylar envelopes, acid-free folders, and pre-cut phase box kits. Some of these items are a bit more costly than the do-it-yourself methods offered here, but often they save enough time to more than offset the expense. Of course, there are other considerations as well. For example, the pre-cut phase box kits are actually cheaper than the board recommended for phase box use. However, these kits also use a 20-point board, about the same thickness as a standard catalog card. While this board is heavy enough for books that still have their boards loosely attached or that do not circulate much, it is not heavy enough to protect a more severely deteriorated book or one that circulates frequently.

Several of the protective enclosures discussed in this chapter utilize polyester film such as Mylar®D or Mellinex®151. This is not simply because polyester film is an extremely versatile material, useful in many preservation procedures. It also offers simple, cost-effective solutions to many preservation problems, and is available in a variety of forms, including mylar envelopes, pre-cut encapsulation units, sheets, and rolls. Some suppliers even offer envelopes with a tab along one side, punched with holes for storage in a photo album or other three-ring binder.

Because one type of object can usually be treated with more than one type of enclosure, this chapter will be divided into two sections. The first will discuss enclosures for three-dimensional objects, like books and AV materials. The second will discuss two-dimensional objects, such as maps and letters. Decisions relating to specific problems will be addressed at the beginning of each section rather than at the beginning of the chapter, and alternative conservation suggestions will be discussed at the end of each section rather than at the end of the chapter.

DECISIONS

The following factors will influence your decision regarding the most appropriate preservation treatment. These factors address first the broader context, then the specific problem(s) to be treated.

BROAD FACTORS

Importance of the item

Physical needs of the object

Desired outcome

Time available

Personnel available for this procedure

Money available

Expertise available

ENCLOSURES FOR THREE-DIMENSIONAL OBJECTS

The difference between alternative enclosures is usually in the degree of protection offered by each enclosure. For example, a book with loose boards might be given a polyester book wrap, which would offer a thin, flexible layer of protection.

TERMINOLOGY FOR DIMENSIONS

In all enclosures for three-dimensional objects, it is important to understand the terminology for dimensions. Three measurements must be taken for three-dimensional objects—the height of the book, the width of the book, and the depth of the book. The height of the book is measured from the top edge of the cover to the bottom edge of the cover. The width of the book is measured from the spine of the cover to the fore edge of the cover. The depth of the book is measured from the front cover to the back cover. It is important to take each measurement in at least two places and to use the larger of these measurements. This accommodates any irregularities of the book (see Figure 52).

Figure 52

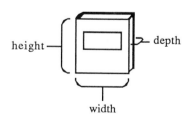

This will be adequate if the book is seldom used or will soon be replaced or repaired. The same book might be given a phase box if it circulates more frequently and will receive no further treatment. The book wrap utilizes tape in close proximity to the book and may be somewhat confusing to patrons. Therefore, it is suggested that you place a notice on the wrap referring the patron to the circulation desk for assistance or restrict its use to closed stack situations.

The following specific factors must be considered:

Degree of protection required for this object,

Further treatment plans for this object, and

Frequency of circulation for this object.

BOOK WRAPS

Book wraps can be made of polyester film or polyethylene, the latter being recommended when the binding is particularly brittle or deteriorated. Book wraps are most often used on books that have loose or separated boards and that are seldom used. Many libraries have a number of books held together with rubber bands or strings. If these books are used infrequently, they are perfect candidates for book wraps. Polyethylene book wraps should be used if pieces of the cover or the paper are fragile enough that the static electricity or sharp edges of the polyester film will further damage the book. Otherwise, polyester film is acceptable for the book wrap.

SUPPLIES

Polyethylene or polyester film

Double-sided tape (¼-inch 3M Scotch Brand® 415)

Bone folder

PROCEDURE

1. Cut a piece of polyethylene or polyester film as wide as the book is tall and long enough to wrap around the book with about two inches of overlap (see Figure 53a).

Figures 53a–c

MAKING A BOOK WRAP

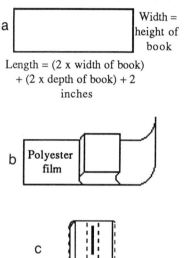

a — Width = height of book

Length = (2 x width of book) + (2 x depth of book) + 2 inches

b — Polyester film

c

Double-sided tape

2. Lay the book in the center of the film, being careful to line up the top and bottom edge of the book with the top and bottom edge of the film. Then wrap the flap on the fore edge side of the book around the front of the book (see Figure 53b).

3. Cut a piece of double-sided tape approximately one inch shorter than the book, and place it on the top of the flap that is resting on the front of the book.

4. Peel off the backing of the tape and wrap the spine side flap around the front of the book, letting it fall on top of the double-sided tape. Gently press the tape with a bone folder or your thumb (see Figure 53c).

BOOK JACKETS

Book jackets are made of polyester film. They are used primarily on books that are somewhat deteriorated but still have attached boards, or on books with special bindings that need extra protection. There are several commercially available book jackets and book jacket systems. Many are made from polyester film, but usually it is a lighter weight (1.5 to 2 mil) than recommended here. However, if you intend to make a large number of book jackets, it may be more feasible to use one of these commercially available systems.

SUPPLIES

Polyester film (3 mil)

Bone folder

Cutting device (large paper cutter, or a ruler and scalpel or X-Acto® knife)

PROCEDURE
1. Cut a piece of polyester film as wide as the book is tall and five times longer than the book's width. It is very important that this piece of polyester film be cut exactly square. You might want to cut the piece a little larger than needed, and then square it up and cut it to the exact size (see Figure 54a).

Figures 54a–b

MAKING A BOOK JACKET

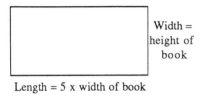

Width = height of book

Length = 5 x width of book

a

Fold #1   Fold #3   Fold #5

| Front Inner Flap | Front Cover | Spine | Back Cover | Back Inner Flap |

Fold #2   Fold #4   Fold #6

b

2. Measuring along one of the long sides of the polyester film, the first fold will be at a distance equal to the inside of the front cover, from gutter to fore edge. Pinch the polyester film at this point to mark it; then fold it over, holding the edges together and gently slide a bone folder along the newly formed crease. Go over the crease more firmly with the bone folder one or two more times.

3. The next crease will be only $\frac{1}{8}$ inch to $\frac{3}{16}$ inch from the first, depending on the thickness of the boards of the book to be covered. It will be easier to make this second crease if the first has been flattened a little with your thumb. After the second crease is made, the two can be formed back into a square.

4. The next crease will be at a distance equal to the outside width of the board, from fore edge to spine edge. Allow the polyester film to curve around the spine if the spine is curved. If you are placing a polyester film jacket on the outside of the original dust jacket, allow enough film to reach to the spine's farthest point. In this case, there will be a small gap between the inner corners of your book jacket and the original dust jacket.

5. Continue to make creases at the other side of the spine and at the fore edge of the back board. Then cut the film so that its end reaches to the gutter inside the back board (see Figure 54b).

POLYESTER PAMPHLET PROTECTOR

The polyester pamphlet protector is composed of two pieces of polyester film: one piece forms an inner sling and the other forms an outer wrap. It can be utilized to protect weak or damaged paperbound books, thin hardbound books, or pamphlets. It is particularly useful when the covers or pages of the book are loose. Not only does this protector help to hold all the loose pieces together; it does not take up as much shelf space as would a phase box or clamshell box.

The following instructions describe a pamphlet protector

for a thin book. These are the most difficult, and pamphlet protectors for smaller items, such as single section pamphlets, utilize the same techniques.

SUPPLIES

Polyester film

Bone folder

Double-sided tape (3M Scotch Brand® 415)

Metal ruler and X-Acto® knife or scalpel

PROCEDURE

1. Measure the book or pamphlet. If you are working with a thin pamphlet ($\frac{3}{16}$ inch or less), you will not need to measure the depth.

2. Cut the inner piece of polyester film. The inner piece of polyester film will be as wide as the width of the book. It will be as long as the height of the book multiplied by two, plus the depth of the book, plus four inches. Use the knife and straightedge to cut the polyester to the desired dimensions (see Figure 55a).

3. Cut the outer piece of polyester film. The outer piece of polyester film will be as wide as the book is high. It will be as long as the width of the book multiplied by two, plus the depth of the book multiplied by two, plus two inches (see Figure 55b).

4. Fold the inner piece of polyester film. All folds in both pieces of polyester will be across the shorter dimension. Beginning at one corner and measuring along one of the long sides of this piece of polyester film, make the first fold at a distance equal to the height of the book plus two inches. Continue measuring from the first fold, and the second fold will be at a distance equal to the depth of the book. If you are making a protector for a thin pamphlet, you only need a single fold. After folding, the two long sections of this piece of film should be approximately equal in length. The fit of this piece can be tested by placing the book inside the folded piece of polyester with the bottom edge of the book resting on the center section of the polyester. The two longer sections should project above the book by about two inches (see Figure 56a).

Figures 55a–b

CUTTING POLYESTER FILM FOR PAMPHLET PROTECTOR

a

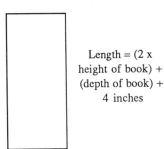

Polyester film

Width = height of book

Length = (2 x width of book) + (2 x depth of book) + 2 inches

Length = (2 x height of book) + (depth of book) + 4 inches

Width = width of book

b

Figures 56a–b

FOLDING INNER PIECE OF POLYESTER FILM

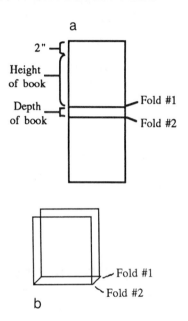

a

2"

Height of book

Depth of book

Fold #1

Fold #2

Fold #1

Fold #2

b

5. Fold the outer piece of polyester film. Beginning at one corner and measuring along one of the long sides, make the first fold at a distance equal to one-half the width of the book, plus one inch. Continue measuring from the first fold and make the second fold at a distance equal to the depth of the book. If you are making a protector for a thin pamphlet, you should only make a single fold. Continuing from the second fold, make the third fold at a distance equal to the width of

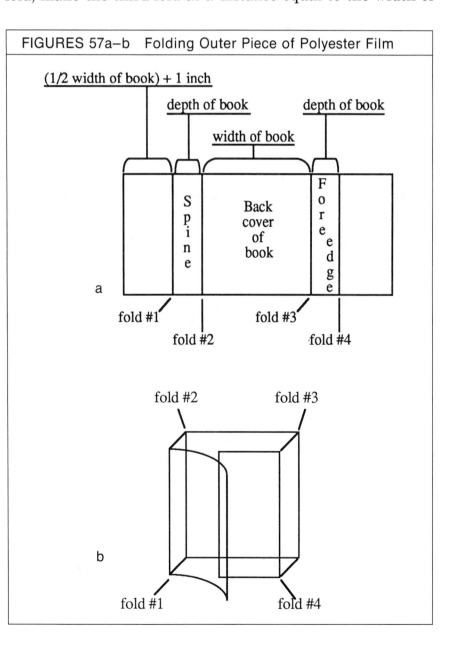

FIGURES 57a–b   Folding Outer Piece of Polyester Film

(1/2 width of book) + 1 inch

depth of book

depth of book

width of book

Spine

Back cover of book

Fore edge

a

fold #1

fold #2

fold #3

fold #4

fold #2

fold #3

b

fold #1

fold #4

Figures 58a–c

ADDING BOTTOM FLAP

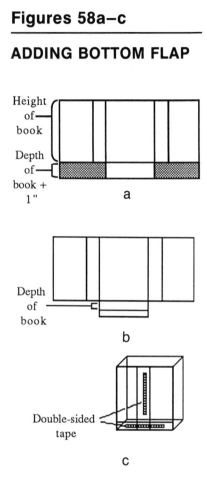

Height of book

Depth of book + 1"

a

Depth of book

b

Double-sided tape

c

the book. Again, if you are making a protector for a thin pamphlet, you should make a single fold, omitting the next fold. The final fold will be at a distance equal to the depth of the book, measured from the third fold. After folding, the two end sections should be approximately equal in length. The fit of this piece of polyester can be tested by wrapping the polyester around the book with the back cover of the book resting on the center section of the polyester. The two end flaps should overlap on the front cover by about two inches (see Figures 57a and b).

6. Tape the outer piece of polyester. With the book inside the inner piece of polyester film, wrap the outer piece around the book and the inner piece of polyester film. The front flap that is folded on the spine side of the book should be on top of the other front flap. If this left flap is lifted off the book, a piece of double-sided tape can be applied to the right flap. When the backing is removed from the tape, the left flap can be dropped onto the tape and pressed into place. The outer piece of film should be tight enough to provide static electricity, which will hold the inner piece of film and the book inside. It should also be loose enough that the inner piece of film and the book can be pulled out through the top without removing the tape on the outer piece.

7. An optional bottom flap can be added to this design for extra strength for use with thicker or heavier books. In order to add this flap, you must alter the measurements for the outer piece of polyester film. Simply add the depth of the book plus one inch to the width of the outer piece of film. Then after the folds are made in the outer piece of film, the shaded areas are cut away with a sharp knife. The remaining flap is folded at a distance equal to the depth of the book. When taping the outer piece of polyester film, add a piece of tape across this bottom flap before taping the right front flap (see Figures 58a-c).

PHASE BOXES

Phase boxes are made out of two pieces of acid-free board that are glued together to form a protective housing, usually for a frequently used book that is losing its boards or even some of its pages (see Figures 59a and b).

Phase boxes are perhaps the most versatile of protective enclosures, as they can be adapted to all types of materials, from videocassettes and other AV materials to photo albums and realia (see Figure 60). They are excellent for holding together groups of items, such as back issues of a magazine that are too brittle to bind, or filmstrips and their accompanying audio cassettes. There are commercial phase box kits available at a fairly reasonable cost. Although they are made of a somewhat lighter board and do not fit as precisely as a handmade box, they are simple to use and can be very useful when only light protection is needed or when a phase box is needed on the spur of the moment.

SUPPLIES

Acid-free barrier or phase box board (approximately .060 inch)

PVA

Glue brush

Ruler

Small velcro fasteners (Velcoins or one-inch-square pieces of velcro tape)

Utility knife and straight edge or metal ruler

Scalpel or X-Acto® knife

Bone folder

Figure 59a

DIAGRAM OF A BASIC PHASE BOX

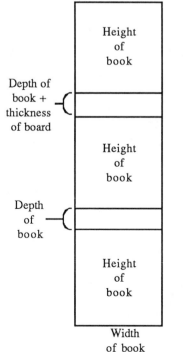

FIGURE 59b Diagram of a Basic Phase Box

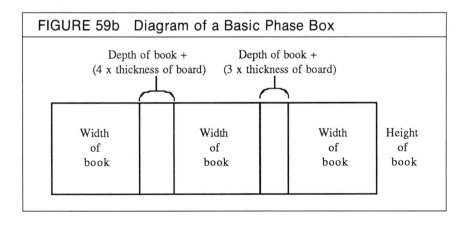

FIGURE 60   Common Types of Phase Boxes

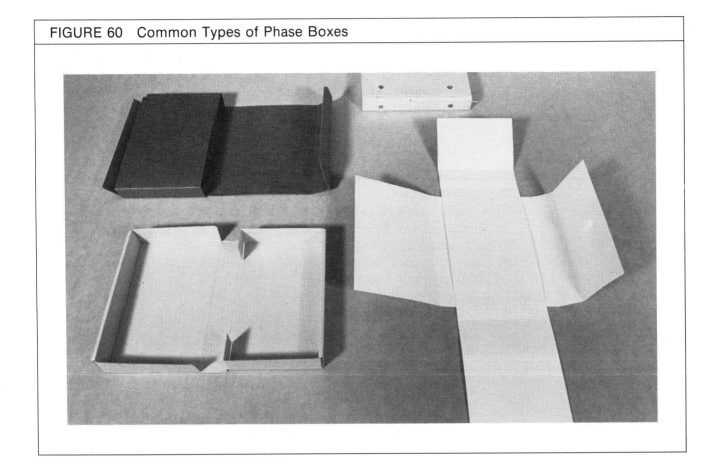

OPTIONAL SUPPLIES

Board shear

Board crimper

PROCEDURE

1. Measure the width of the book and, using the utility knife and straightedge, cut a strip of board that is as wide as the book. Its length should be equal to three times the height of the book, plus twice the depth of the book, plus the thickness of the board you are using. It is good, however, to cut the board a little longer than this and trim it later. This strip will form the inner piece of the phase box. It is important that the grain of the board be parallel to the short sides of the strip (see Figure 61a).

2. Place the book on one end of the inner board, and make a mark on the board $\frac{1}{16}$ inch past the length of the book. The thickness of the board you are using will determine the exact distance for this measurement. Some experimentation may be necessary to find the measurement need, but $\frac{1}{16}$ inch is a good starting point (see Figure 61b).

Figures 61a–e

FOLDING INNER BOARD

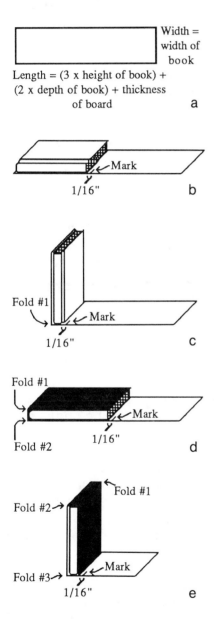

Width = width of book

Length = (3 x height of book) + (2 x depth of book) + thickness of board

a

Mark

1/16"

b

Fold #1

Mark

1/16"

c

Fold #1

Mark

1/16"

Fold #2

d

Fold #1

Fold #2→

Mark

Fold #3→

1/16"

e

3. Remove the book and, with the bone folder, score the board in a line parallel to the short edge of the board and even with the mark on the board. Turn the board over and, with the scalpel, gently score this side of the board on exactly the same line. Be sure not to cut too deeply, or the crease will tear out. If you are using a board crimper, simply crimp the board parallel to the short edge of the board and even with the mark on the board.

4. Lay the book on the flap you have just made and hold the book against the flap as you stand the book up. Place a mark on the board $\frac{1}{16}$ inch past the exposed cover of the book. Remove the book and score the board on a line through your new mark and parallel to the first crease, using the bone folder on the inside and the scalpel on the outside (see Figure 61c).

5. Replace the book on the board and fold these first two creases; then place a mark $\frac{1}{16}$ inch past the end of the book. Remove the book and score as previously described, parallel to the other creases and through the new mark (see Figure 61d).

6. Replace the book on the board and fold the first three creases; then place a mark $\frac{1}{16}$ inch past the first flap, the edge of which should be touching the board. If you wish to double-check this measurement, it should be equal to the thickness of the book, plus the thickness of the board, plus $\frac{1}{16}$ inch. Remove the book and score (see Figure 61e).

7. Replace the book on the board and fold all creases to wrap the board around the book. Place a mark on the board even with the end of this package. Remove the book and cut the board through this mark. Some people prefer to make this cut $\frac{1}{2}$-inch closer to the last crease rather than exactly through the mark. The inner board is now completed.

8. Cut a strip of board as wide as the book is tall, plus three times the thickness of the board. Its length should be three times the width of the book, plus two times the depth of the book, plus seven times the thickness of the board. Again, the grain of the board should be parallel to the short sides of the strip. This will be the outer board of the phase box (see Figure 62a).

Figures 62a–e

FOLDING OUTER BOARD

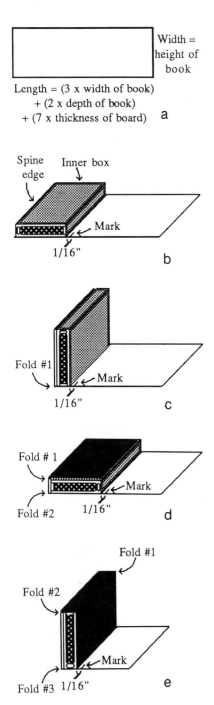

Width = height of book

Length = (3 x width of book)
+ (2 x depth of book)
+ (7 x thickness of board)   a

Spine edge   Inner box

Mark

1/16"   b

Fold #1

Mark

1/16"   c

Fold # 1

Mark

Fold #2   1/16"   d

Fold #1

Fold #2

Mark

Fold #3 1/16"   e

9. Place the box formed by the folded inner board on the right end of the outer board, and place a mark $\frac{1}{16}$ inch past the end of the inner box. Remove the inner box and score the outer board, parallel to the short sides of the board and through your mark (see Figure 62b).

10. Replace the inner box and fold the first flap of the outer board up; then place a mark on the outer board $\frac{1}{16}$ inch past the edge of the inner box. Remove the inner box and score the outer board (see Figure 62c).

11. Replace the inner box and fold the first two creases of the outer board; then place a mark on the outer board $\frac{1}{16}$ inch past the edge of the inner box. Remove the inner box and score the outer board (see Figure 62d).

12. Replace the inner box and fold the first three creases of the outer board; then place a mark on the outer board $\frac{1}{16}$ inch past the first flap of the outer board. Remove the inner box and score the outer board (see Figure 62e).

13. Replace the inner box; fold all creases on the outer box; and place a mark on the outer board where the first crease touches it. Remove the inner box and cut the outer board parallel to the creases and through your last mark.

14. Cut $\frac{1}{4}$ inch to $\frac{1}{2}$ inch off the corners of each board at a 45° angle or use a Corner Rounder to remove the sharp corners of the boards.

15. Brush PVA on the scored side of the center panel of the outer board. Place the center panel of the cut side of the inner board on this glued section. Make sure the edges line up squarely so that the creases can be easily folded. Then open the phase box and weight the glued section until the PVA is dry (see Figure 63a-c).

16. When the PVA has dried, close the phase box and attach the velcro fasteners. Remove the adhesive covering from one side of the fasteners and fix them to the small end flap of the outer box about one inch in from each end. When they are attached to the flap, remove the adhesive covering for the other side of the velcro and close the flap around the box, applying pressure to the velcro for a few seconds.

Figures 63a–c

GLUING THE INNER BOX

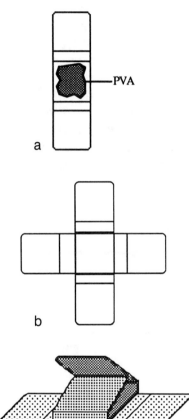

a

b

c

ALTERNATIVE CONSERVATION SUGGESTIONS

Items of historical or artistic value often require more durable and more aesthetically pleasing enclosures than those discussed above. For instance, rare books that are candidates for book wraps or phase boxes because of their deteriorated state are also candidates for the more complicated clamshell box. The Library of Congress offers complete instructions for several variations of the clamshell box in *Boxes for the Protection of Rare Books: Their Design and Construction*. Several companies, such as Conservation Resources, BookLab, and many commercial binders offer clamshell boxes made to order for each book. However, this can be expensive. Another alternative is full conservation treatment, which brings the book as nearly as possible to a completely stable state. Ironically, the cost of this treatment is often great enough that, afterwards, a library opts to have a clamshell box made to protect the book anyway.

ENCLOSURES FOR TWO-DIMENSIONAL OBJECTS

The most common enclosures for two-dimensional objects are acid-free folders, encapsulation, and lamination or dry mounting. Differences between these enclosures include the level of reversibility and the degree of harm done to the object. Lamination and dry mounting require the application of heat, and the use of an adhesive directly on the object. Both of these processes cause irreversible damage to the object. A map could be encapsulated, which is entirely reversible. The same map might be laminated, an irreversible process that can actually hasten the deterioration of the item it will be protecting.

Lamination and dry mounting are two of the few alternatives to encapsulation; therefore, you might have to choose among these procedures often. Though frowned upon by most conservators, lamination and dry mounting can offer advantages over encapsulation in some situations, and there are many cases when it can be very useful in the library. For example, a current U.S. map, which is used as a teaching aid, is a good candidate for lamination or dry mounting. These processes not only provide a tough, durable enclosure, but they also provide a surface that can be written on with wax pencil, then wiped clean, and written on again. Another example would be a reader's copy of a county or state map that will be replaced as soon as it is superseded by a newer map. Lamination and dry mounting can also be useful in creating temporary or permanent signage in a library, or to protect posters that will be used as decorations. Conversely, lamination and dry mounting should never be considered for maps, documents, or other objects of artistic or historic value. The following specific factors must be considered when choosing an enclosure for two-dimensional objects.

Intended use of this object

Size of this object

Number of printed sides on this object

MAKING AN ACID-FREE FOLDER

A folder is the simplest form of enclosure for two-dimensional objects. It can be made from virtually any type of acid-free, and preferably lignin-free, board. In general, a wide range of board weights, or thicknesses, is acceptable. The board must be strong enough and stiff enough to protect the object from abrasion and accidental creasing or folding. The thinnest available board that meets these criteria is usually best because it will take up less room in your flat file storage area. Light- or medium-weight Bristol board, two-ply mat board, and light-weight barrier board can all be used to make an acid-free folder.

A more important consideration is the acid content of the board. The preferred board in any case will be acid-free and lignin-free; however, some boards are buffered with an agent that allows the board to absorb a certain amount of acid before it becomes acidic itself. This means that the board will last longer when it is adjacent to an acidic object such as an old letter. While buffering is good for the storage of most paper objects, it is not always good for photographs. Unbuffered, but still acid-free and lignin-free, board should be used with most photographs and negatives because the buffering agents can chemically react with these objects in harmful ways. Buffered boards should be used only with very brittle photographs and certain types of early prints and films. If you have any old photographs that you are concerned about, it is suggested that you contact a photograph conservator.

Most library vendors offer a full line of acid-free folders, ranging from file folders for small objects to map and poster folders for objects as large as 32 inches by 40 inches. Many vendors even offer both buffered and unbuffered versions of these folders. Depending upon your resources, these commercially available folders can be a very good alternative to creating your own folders.

The primary disadvantage in using folders for storage is that the two flaps of folders are joined only on one side. While this allows easy access, it does not protect the object as well as encapsulation would. For example, when a folder is moved too quickly, the object inside can slide partially or completely out of the folder. Since it is possible for the object to move around inside the folder, it is possible for the object to get damaged. One other disadvantage is that folders take up slightly more space than would encapsulated objects. In some situations it is best to use a combination of encapsulation and acid-free folders. For example, several related and individually encapsulated objects might all be kept in one acid-free folder. This combination does not take up as much room as keeping each item in its own folder, yet it gives the added protection of encapsulation to each object.

SUPPLIES

Acid-free board

Metal ruler and X-Acto® Knife or scalpel

Bone folder

PROCEDURE

1. Measure the height and width of the object. Add six to eight inches to each measurement. This will allow three to four inches of border around the object and will be the size of the completed folder.

Figures 64a–c

MEASURING AND SCORING AN ACID-FREE FOLDER

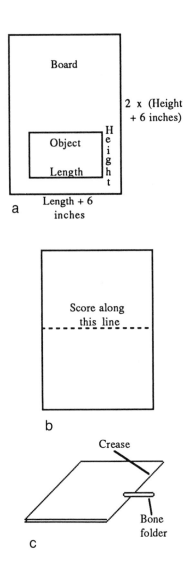

a

b

c

2. Cut a piece of board for the folder. It should be twice the size of the completed folder in one direction so that it can be folded over (see Figure 64a). It is best to make the crease on one of the long sides of the object. If the object is longer than it is tall, you will make the crease at the top. If it is taller than it is long, you will make the crease on the left side. It is best if the grain of the board runs parallel to the crease. This is not always possible, however, with larger objects.

3. Use the ruler to locate and mark the half-way point on the long sides of the board. The line between these points is where the crease will be formed.

4. Use the ruler and the bone folder to score the board along this center line on the side of the board that will be the inside of the folder (see Figure 64b).

5. Try to fold the board along the scored line. If it does not bend easily, the board is too thick to be scored on one side only. You will need to score the outside of the board along the same line with the X-Acto® knife or scalpel. Be very careful not to cut all the way through the board. You want to cut only the outer layers of the board.

6. When the board folds easily, close the folder and rub the outside of the crease with the bone folder (see Figure 64c).

ENCAPSULATION

Encapsulations are made of two pieces of polyester film, one behind the object and one in front, which are attached along two or more edges. The edges of this package may be sealed with heat or sonar welders, but double-sided tape is acceptable if you cannot afford one of these expensive machines. Encapsulation is used for flat items, such as documents, maps, posters, or prints that are damaged, brittle, or needing overall protection because of frequent use. It is particularly useful for items that have printing on both sides or large items that would be awkward to laminate. Encapsulation should not be used on charcoal, pastel drawings, or graphite, as these items have very loose pigments that can be pulled off the surface of the paper by the static electricity of the polyester film.

If the item selected for encapsulation could benefit from cleaning, it is wise to do so before it is encapsulated. See Chapter 2 for paper cleaning procedures.

OPTIONAL SUPPLIES

Measuring grid

Squeegee

Scissors

Cotton gloves

SUPPLIES

Polyester film

Double-sided tape (¼-inch 3M Scotch Brand® 415)

Bone folder

Weights

Soft bristled brush (such as a hake brush or a photography brush)

Cutting device (metal ruler and X-Acto® knife or scalpel)

PROCEDURE

Throughout this procedure, it is preferable that the polyester film be handled only on the extreme edges which will not come into contact with the item itself. If you find this difficult, you may use cotton gloves and handle the polyester film more freely.

1. Lay the item out on a smooth, clean, and dry surface and lightly dust the item with a soft bristled brush. Turn the item over and dust the back in the same manner.

2. Measure the item; then cut two pieces of polyester film approximately two inches larger than the item. Lay one piece on a clean, dry surface. Some people prefer to use a measuring grid as a work surface. Grids are available in many sizes with various units of measurement and can be helpful in measuring the item and the polyester as well as in centering the item on the polyester.

3. Lay the item face down on this piece of polyester film with approximately one inch of film extending beyond the item's edges on all sides. Place a small weight on a piece of scrap polyester film in the center of the item to hold it in place.

4. Place a piece of double-sided tape on the polyester film

Figures 65a–b

BASIC ENCAPSULATING PROCEDURE

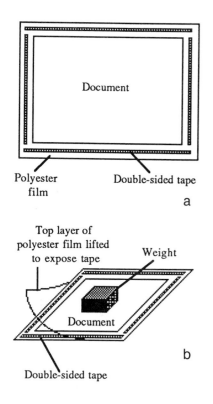

Polyester film

Double-sided tape

a

Top layer of polyester film lifted to expose tape

Weight

Document

Double-sided tape

b

about ¼ inch away from and parallel to each side of the item. Leave small spaces between the ends of the strips of tape (see Figure 65a).

5. Remove the weight, and place the second piece of polyester film on top of the item. Then, replace the weight, making sure the item is still square on the film between the strips of tape.

6. While gently holding one corner of the top piece of polyester film, remove the backing from the tape on two adjacent sides of the item (see Figure 65b). Let the film drop into place. Use the squeegee to force extra air out of the encapsulation.

7. Repeat the above step on the remaining strips of tape; use the squeegee once again to force out whatever air is left in the encapsulation.

8. Trim the edges of the polyester film to within approximately ¼ inch of the tape. Trim the corners of the polyester to a round shape with a scalpel or scissors to avoid damaging other items (or yourself) with the sharp corners.

LAMINATION AND DRY MOUNTING

Lamination is the process of mounting a poster, map, or print to a clear, adhesive film. Both sides of the document are protected with this method. Dry mounting is the process of attaching a flat object to a stiff backing material by means of an adhesive film. Laminates and dry mounting films come in two basic forms, those with pressure-sensitive adhesives and those that require both heat and pressure to activate the adhesive. The heat-sensitive adhesive films require a roll laminator or a larger drymount/laminating press. These processes can also be combined to produce a tough, durable package with a stiff backing material and a protective laminate on the front.

Most library vendors offer several types of films for both laminating and dry mounting. These films come in a variety of weights, finishes, and adhesive types. For example, the adhesive on some pressure-sensitive films is repositionable, while some adhesives set almost instantly. Most heat-sensitive films are permanent, but some vendors do offer *archival* or reversible laminates. It should be remembered, however, that heat-sensitive adhesive films do require heat, which contributes to the deterioration of paper objects, and the reversal of heat-sensitive films also requires the application of either heat or chemicals. Any time you use a process that requires heat, you will be doing some irreversible damage to the object.

The following instructions are for application of heat-sensitive adhesive films with a dry mount/laminating press. This is the most complicated method of laminating or dry mounting, but the application of pressure-sensitive films utilizes many of the same techniques.

LAMINATION

SUPPLIES

Laminating film

Release paper

Rigid board

Weights

Metal ruler and X-Acto® knife or scalpel

Roll laminator or dry mount/laminating press

Squeegee or brayer

PROCEDURE

1. If you are using a press or a roll laminator, set the temperature to the level suggested for the film, usually between 210° F and 275° F. Be sure to use the manufacturer's recommended temperature; a few degrees can be the difference between protecting an object and destroying it.

2. Put the object in the press and close the press for about ten seconds to ensure that the object is completely dry.

3. Cut two pieces of laminating film that are slightly larger than the object to be laminated.

Figures 66a–b

BASIC LAMINATING PROCEDURE

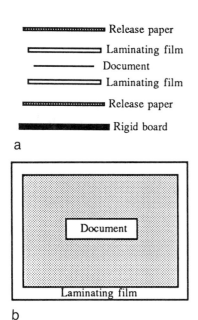

Release paper
Laminating film
Document
Laminating film
Release paper
Rigid board

a

Document

Laminating film

b

4. Place the materials in the press in the order illustrated in Figure 66a. Make sure the laminating film and object are lined up, with the film overlapping the object on all sides (see Figure 66b).

5. Heat this package in the press for the length of time suggested by the manufacturer of your film. Times usually range from 30 seconds to five or six minutes. As with the temperature, the incorrect time can spell disaster, not only for the object being laminated, but for the press as well.

6. Carefully remove the package (it will be hot) from the press and cool under a weight. The rigid board used earlier in the press can be used for this purpose as well. If there are bubbles or creases in the laminating film, place the object on a hard, flat surface and use a squeegee or brayer to gently force the bubbles to the edge of the laminate or to gently stretch the laminate until creases are removed.

7. When the object has cooled, use the ruler and knife to trim the edges of the laminating film, leaving a ⅛-inch to ¼-inch margin around the object.

DRY MOUNTING

Sometimes a piece of plywood, pressboard, or foamcore is used in place of the back piece of film to provide a stiffer backing. While dry mounting is very similar to laminating, there are a few differences. First, the two processes require different types of adhesive films. Dry mount film has adhesive on both sides, whereas laminating film has adhesive on only one side. Second, dry mounting does not require the use of a rigid board underneath the package when in the press. The backing material is usually rigid enough, and most dry mount adhesives do not require the same amount of pressure that lamination does. Third, lamination requires that the adhesive film overlap the object in order to ensure a good seal. Dry mounting allows you the option of cutting the backing material down to the exact size of the object or leaving the backing material larger, overlapping the object and forming a margin around it. The latter technique is necessary if you intend to put a laminating film on the front of an item that will be dry mounted because the laminating film must overlap the object. When this combination of processes is undertaken, mount the object first, then apply the laminating film.

SUPPLIES

Dry mount film

Backing material (plywood, press board, or foamcore)

Release paper

Metal ruler and X-Acto® knife or scalpel

Dry mount/laminating press

Weights

Tacking iron if necessary

PROCEDURE

1. Heat the press to the suggested temperature, usually 210° F to 275° F, and cut a piece of the backing material that is slightly larger than the desired size. Be sure to follow the manufacture's recommended temperature. A few degrees can be the difference between protecting an object and destroying it.

2. Cut a piece of dry mount adhesive film slightly larger than the object. If the backing material will be trimmed to the size of the object, proceed to step 5. If the backing material will be left larger than the object, follow steps 3 and 4.

3. Lay the object face down on a flat surface. Place the adhesive film on the back of the object and a piece of release paper on top of that. Using the tacking iron on a medium heat, tack the adhesive film to the object at one spot along two opposite edges (see Figure 67a).

4. Remove the release paper and turn the object face up with the dry mount film lightly attached. Then, using the ruler and knife, trim the dry mount adhesive film to the edges of the item, being careful not to cut the item as well.

Figures 67a–b

BASIC DRY MOUNTING PROCEDURE

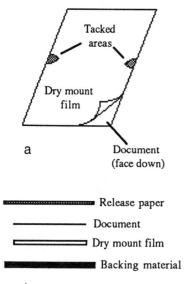

a

b

5. Place the materials in the press in the order illustrated in Figure 67b. Be sure that the object, the adhesive, and the backing material are correctly aligned in the press.

6. Heat this package in the press for the suggested length of time, usually 10 to 60 seconds.

7. Remove the object from the press and cool under weights.

8. When the object is cool, trim the backing material to the desired size. If it is to be the exact size of the object, you will be trimming the excess adhesive at the same time.

ALTERNATIVE CONSERVATION SUGGESTIONS

There are two enclosure options available for two-dimensional objects that are not discussed in this chapter. The first option is housing the object in a mat made from archival mat board. This option is particularly desirable for objects of value, which are printed on one side only and will be exhibited from time to time. The second option is lining the object with a thin, sturdy, archival backing material such as Japanese paper. This is a very tricky process and should not be undertaken by anyone but experienced conservators.

FURTHER READINGS

Phase Boxes:

Brown, pp. 1–35.

Kyle, pp. 95–118.

Encapsulation:

Greenfield, pp. 83–89.

Morrow, pp. 117–122.

APPENDIX A: SUPPLIES

BINDERS (FOLDERS)
Brodart, Demco, Gaylord, LBS, Light Impressions, University Products

BOARD
Barrier (Phase box): Conservation Resources, LBS, University Products

Binders (Davey): BookMakers, Conservation Resources, LBS, TALAS, University Products

Bristol: University Products

BONE FOLDERS
BookMakers, Brodart, TALAS, University Products

BOOK CLOTH
BookMakers, TALAS, University Products

BOOK COVERS (READY MADE)
Brodart, Demco, Gaylord, Highsmith, Kapco

BOXES
Archival Storage: Bill Cole, Brodart, Conservation Resources, Highsmith, Hollinger, Light Impressions, TALAS, University Products

Clamshell (rare book): Conservation Resources

Phase (ready-made or custom-made): Conservation Resources, University Products

BRUSHES
BookMakers, Brodart, Demco, Gaylord, TALAS, University Products

CLEANERS
Absorene: Brodart, Demco, Gaylord, TALAS, University Products

Document Cleaning Pad: Brodart, Demco, Gaylord, Highsmith, TALAS, University Products

CLOTH
Book: BookMakers, TALAS, University Products

Jaconet: BookMakers

Super (cotton, linen): BookMakers, TALAS, University Products

Tape: Brodart, Demco, Gaylord, Highsmith, TALAS, University Products

ENCAPSULATION KITS
Brodart, Demco, Gaylord, University Products

ERASERS
Compound: Boise Cascade, Demco, Gaylord

Gum: Boise Cascade, Brodart, Demco, Gaylord, University Products

Kneaded rubber: Boise Cascade, Demco, University Products

Plastic/vinyl: Boise Cascade, Demco, Gaylord

GLUE
Book: Brodart, Demco, Gaylord, Highsmith

Polyvinyl acetate (acid-free): BookMakers, Brodart, Gaylord, Highsmith, Kapco, TALAS, University Products

HEATING (TACKING) IRON
Brodart, Demco, Highsmith, Light Impressions, TALAS, University Products

HEAT-SET TISSUE
BookMakers, TALAS, University Products

NONWOVEN (SPUN) POLYESTER
BookMakers, TALAS, University Products

PAPER
Blotting: BookMakers, Light Impressions, University Products

End sheets: BookMakers, Conservation Resources, Demco, Gaylord, Light Impressions, TALAS, University Products

Japanese: BookMakers, Highsmith, TALAS, University Products

Marbled: BookMakers, Light Impressions, TALAS, University Products

Release: BookMakers, Brodart, Demco, Gaylord, Light Impressions, TALAS, University Products

Tissue: Conservation Resources, Demco, Light Impressions, TALAS, University Products

Waxed: Brodart, Demco, Gaylord

PASTE
Book: Brodart, Demco, Gaylord

Methyl Cellulose: BookMakers, Light Impressions, TALAS, University Products

Rice: TALAS, University Products

Wheat: BookMakers, Light Impressions, TALAS, University Products

POLYESTER FILM
Envelopes: Bill Cole, Demco, Conservation Resources, Highsmith, Light Impressions, TALAS, University Products

Rolls: Demco, Highsmith, Light Impressions, TALAS, University Products

Sheets: BookMakers, Demco, Conservation Resources, Gaylord, Highsmith, Light Impressions, TALAS, University Products

TAPE
Archival (Document) Repair: Brodart, Bill Cole, Gaylord, Highsmith, Light Impressions, TALAS, University Products

Book Mending: Brodart, Demco, Gaylord, Kapco, University Products

  Hinge: Brodart, Demco, Kapco, University Products

  Paper: Brodart, Demco, Gaylord, Kapco, Light Impressions, University Products

  Spine: Brodart, Demco, Gaylord, Kapco

  Wings: Brodart, Demco, Gaylord, Kapco

Double-sided: Brodart, Gaylord

3M Scotch® 415: Conservation Resources, Demco, Gaylord, Highsmith, Light Impressions, TALAS, University Products

THREAD (BINDER'S)
BookMakers, Brodart, Demco, Gaylord, TALAS, University Products

APPENDIX B: SUPPLIERS

Bill Cole Enterprises, Inc.
P.O. Box 60
Randolph, MA 02368
(617) 986-2653

Boise Cascade
6601 Universal Avenue
Kansas City, MO 64120
(800) 821-8586

BookMakers, Inc.
6001 66th Avenue, Suite 101
Riverdale, MD 20737
(301) 459-3384

Brodart Co.
1609 Memorial Ave.
Williamsport, PA 17705
(800) 233-8959

Conservation Resources International
8000 H Forbes Place
Springfield, VA 22151
(800) 634-6932

Demco
P.O. Box 7488
Madison, WI 53707
(800) 356-1200

Gaylord Bros., Inc.
Box 4901
Syracuse, NY 13221
(800) 448-6160

The Highsmith Co., Inc.
W5527 Highway 106
Fort Atkinson, WI 53538
(800) 558-2110

Hollinger Corporation
P.O. Box 6185
3810 South Four Mile Run Dr.
Arlington, VA 22206
(703) 671-6600

Kapco
P.O. Box 626
Kent, OH 44240
(800) 843-5368

LBS/Archival Products
2134 Grand Avenue
Des Moines, IA 50305
(800) 247-5323

Light Impressions Corp.
439 Monroe Avenue
Rochester, NY 14607
(800) 828-6216

Preservation Emporium
P.O. Box 226309 Dept. C
Dallas, TX 75222-6309
(214) 331-8902

Process Materials Corp.
301 Veterans Blvd.
P.O. Box 368
Rutherford, NJ 07070
(201) 935-2900

Talas
213 W. 35th Street
New York, NY 10001
(212) 736-7744

University Products
517 Main Street
P.O. Box 101
Holyoke, MA 01041
(800) 628-1912